The Paradox
of Lucid Dreaming

The Paradox
of Lucid Dreaming

A metaphysical theory of mind

Dr Rory Mac Sweeney

Swift publishing

Dedicated to Pinar, my true north in a world without end

Swift Publishing Ltd,
145-157, St John Street,
London,
EC1V 4PW

First published by Swift Publishing in October 2015

ISBN: 978-1-911032-00-7

Contents

Prologue

A Dream of Paradox

One bright day in the darkness of night, a dream of
  paradox began to take flight.
The time was now, the place was here and all it seemed
  was very, very clear.
Half of you went left, half went right, some went black
  and the rest went white,
Up and down, smile and frown, a world of opposites you
  had sown
And as the dreamer created the dream, the dream created
  the dreamer, one was two and that two was you,
A self and another, a father and a mother, and yet one thing
  stood true, that behind all this mystery there still lies the
  indomitable question of you.
As you journey into your dream, nothing is ever quite
  what it seems
Endless direction, meandering correction, a boundless
  maze, a tiring craze,
Stumble and fall, you almost lose it all till something inside
  says,
'Hey! Don't you recall?'
And so the journey begins once more, the time is now, the
  place is here and nobody is really keeping score ...

The plight of the poet, it seems, is to speak the unspeakable, to write that which cannot be transcribed and to shine a light on this mystery that we so casually call life. As we cast the net of our imagination over the millennia of human civilisation, we haul in many exotic ideas, but there is one which forces us into endless debate, one whose very purpose is to perplex us: the paradox. Defined as an apparent contradiction which may also be true, it haunts the philosopher's mind, but it is a hurdle that we must nonetheless jump if we are ever to raise our game to the transcendental dimension that we hope may await us at the end of time.

In many ways, the world we live in is simple because it is made up of a matrix of opposites – black has white, up has down and I have you. It's wonderful; a harmonious symphony of everything and nothing. But between the opposites there lies a dark secret, an ever-gazing witness, the one who perceives the apparent polarities and that is us conscious beings.

To suggest that the world is an objective place would be to insinuate that black means black and white means white, but we only ever see shades of grey because reality is a function of us conscious observers and the means through which we witness it. What I am alluding to here is what we, in the Western world, have been taught to dismiss – a subjective world in which things are not made of hard facts, but only of perception. That is to say that we may not be living in a solid structure, but in some kind of dream.

One usually distinguishes dreaming from reality by virtue of the fact that dreams are normally encountered by our disoriented mind. The dreamer is defined by his or her inability to navigate their world with adequate cognitive function. To dream is to be dizzy; it is to lack direction in the eternal maze of space and time. But what captures my attention is not how dissimilar dreaming is to our waking world; on the contrary, dreams feel real. They feel so real that I dare not suggest they are anything but real and yet we dismiss them as mere trivial by-products of the imagination.

Our current understanding of the world has arisen from our desire to reduce it to a single source. To the scientist, all matter must come from a ubiquitous structure. This building block of all beings, it is proposed, should be tangible and solid but is it? Common sense tells us that there is indeed a world 'out there', we perceive it through the constant flood of input from our five senses but the cosmos is, to quote J.B. Haladane, 'not just queerer than we imagine but queerer than we can imagine'. He was no doubt pointing to the limitations of our senses and our consequential idea of the world.

The mind offers us the ultimate paradox in this existential essay. We can only ever perceive our bodies in our minds and yet our reductionist view suggests that we need a body in order to have a mind. Where was this body before there was a mind to perceive it, could there possibly have been a mind before there was ever a body. Perhaps the body could be a product of mind?

Our Western scientific model suggests that our minds are an illusory mechanism of carbon based biology and that chemistry, when sufficiently complex, yields consciousness, yet this tells us nothing of where this chemistry was before we consciously perceived it unless we adopt the posture of history – that everything that we experience was preceded by another event. On the surface this seems to solve the problem until we dig deep enough into the past and hit a peculiar philosophical wall, known as *infinite regress*. If we take our intuitive view that everything comes from something else and thus creates the trajectory of history backwards in time, then we must eventually ask where the universe itself springs from? Even if we do answer this question, we are ultimately forced to ask where this alleged source came from and so on to infinity. And thus our attempt to reduce the cosmos to a single objective event tends to run aground.

Contrary to the convention of classical cosmology, the advent of quantum physics in our world has rocked our thinking as we are forced to consider that our view of reality may be fashioned by the lens of our observing consciousness. Our attempt to separate the object of our attention from our subjective perspective is proving futile. Our glorious building block, the atom, is falling into the ambiguous realm of imagination as we discover it to be more of a reflection of how we measure it than a thing in its own right.

The line between the physical and the dream world is thinning with every new discovery but one event eclipses all others: the paradox of the lucid dream. In this state, one can become aware of the fact that one is dreaming while dreaming, allowing the dreamer to explore the depths of their own imagination. It is as if one is awake and dreaming at the same time, two states of consciousness that were previously considered antithetical.

Although it is a difficult state to achieve, it is nonetheless apparent that we are building a bridge from the waking to the dream world, a construction which will one day be sufficiently stable to for us to cross on a regular basis. As a lucid dreamer myself, I have spent many hours asleep on my back, yet paradoxically alert and awake, flying around the galaxy. However it is not mere fun and fantasy that I have pursued in this state, but deep knowledge, as the lucid dream has proved to be, for me, the ultimate testing ground for my theory that reality itself is neither objective nor reducible, but in fact a spectrum of pure possibility that is affected by the very thing that perceives it, which is, paradoxically, ourselves.

In the same way that the one cannot separate the dreamer from the dream, I propose that we, the occupants of our physical world, are hopelessly entangled in its very existence and that it comes and goes as our attention engages or withdraws and is only as simple or complex as we perceive it to be. So perhaps we are already living in a kind of dream, and all that is left for us to do is to become more aware of this possibility. In doing so, we would be creating a more lucid cosmos, one which is sensing itself though our eyes and our ears and interpreting itself through our thoughts and actions.

In this book, I offer a meta-theory of consciousness that encompasses activity across all states, including our ordinary waking state and dreaming, as well as others, such as schizophrenia, psychedelics and lucid dreaming. I propose that these states are not, as we have historically regarded them, a quirk of our consciousness, but part of a vast spectrum that pivots around a central focal point I refer to as Factor X.

Throughout the book, I offer my own take on Factor X as I take the reader through my journey of self-discovery from my earliest enquiry through my experimental years to my current view.

This book is not a scientific essay but an invitation to enter into a dialogue with your world in the same way as I have, in the hope that together we will build a better future in which altered states of consciousness move from the periphery of public opinion to play a more central role in our understanding of our place in the cosmos.

As we descend into a more interconnected, hyper-technical age, it is becoming increasingly apparent to us that we are experiencing a paradigm shift in our perception. The universe is expressing more novel information in a single minute than it did in a whole millennium when we first set out on our journey some 13.7 billion years ago. As the climax approaches, it feels as though we, the orphans of the stars, will finally come to know who we are and why we are here and the answer, as will I suggest, lies not on a slab in some science lab but, in truth, on the other side of paradox.

The Paradox of Lucid Dreaming

1) Wake Up, You Are Dreaming

I have some wonderful news for you, something so incredible that I just had to share it. Are you ready? Wait a moment. Are you certain you want to hear it? OK, here goes then … Right now, at this very moment, though it may seem impossible, you are, in fact, dreaming.

Yes, I know how delightful this is. In the realm of dreams, you are a limitless being with infinite possibilities, what could be more exciting? The world is a playground, you can indulge in endless fantasies and they all feel completely real. In fact, they feel so real that you sometimes forget you are dreaming, which makes them even more exciting.

Dreams can be sad too though, even difficult occasionally, but the pain gives meaning to the pleasure. Everything has its opposite – day has night, dark has light, left has right and you have me. Yes, the other half of you is my own self. Together we are one and that one is the dream of life.

There is a catch, however. It is easy to enjoy the dream so much that you actually get lost and believe that it is too real to be a dream. But how could something be 'too real' to be a dream? Aren't dreams real too? This is a very curious question indeed: how can we ever know what is real? Perhaps it isn't possible, but that doesn't stop us from trying. Learning how the world works is what makes life interesting as it allows us to interact with what we see around us in all sorts of wondrous ways.

Being 'awake' in the dream doesn't necessarily change the dream, it changes you and your perception of the dream, but because you are the dream, pretty soon the dream starts to change too. You begin to see the world as it truly is: a reflection of you. It behaves and acts as you think it should. Some people call this karma but I like to call it 'you and I'. People who know they are dreaming while they are dreaming are called *lucid dreamers*. Some such dreamers are so awake that they know the entire world is an extension of their being, just as much as they are an expression of it. What an incredible feeling, to know that you are here, now, masquerading as a self and other, lost in the illusion of space and time, discovering yourself, challenging and changing every corner of the cosmos with your ever-growing array of ideas and technology.

I am a lucid dreamer and I have been awake in the dream for some time now. I love being awake, things feel exactly the same, except that they feel completely different too. I no longer feel that the world is happening to me, it is simply happening. I am it and it is me. There is a world that I inhabit and yet somehow that world is in me. I feel alive and intrigued by the mystery of my own being. I want you to join me here in my dream. Just think how wonderful that would be, knowing that we are both lucid in our dream of life. How might we treat each other, knowing that we are both sharing this experience?

I hope you will join me in this waking dream. We could have an amazing adventure. It is free to join, but we do have a pretty strict dress code; that is, how you wear your mind. Some people wear it closed and tight while others prefer it to be far more open. To get into this dream club, you just have to be willing to let go of everything you think you are and ready to accept that anything is possible. After all, dreams are limitless and so are you.

That's a big ask. I know because I too was scared when I first discovered the secret of the dream. I was so scared I wanted to pretend to myself that I didn't actually know that I was dreaming, so I tried to forget about it. But there are some things that, once known, cannot be unknown. But I'm not talking about belief here; this is far bigger than belief. It is akin to knowing that you are here right now. It is not prey to the possible fallibility of belief. But don't take my word for it; after all, that would constitute believing.

The Paradox of Dreaming

The crux of this dilemma is that if you were dreaming the dream that you were awake, believing that dreams are something that happen when you close your eyes at night-time, then you would be dreaming the 'dream of being awake'. If, on the other hand, you were aware that you were dreaming while you were dreaming, you would really be awake or lucid in the dream. *So if you think you are awake, then actually you are dreaming, and if you know you are dreaming, then really you are awake.* What a conundrum! How could we ever expect to make any sense of this quandary?

That is what we call a paradox — an apparently irresolvable contradiction — and I, for one, love paradoxes. On the surface, paradoxes are puzzling and, as far as scientists and philosophers are concerned, grounds for a good argument. But the cosmic joke is on them for taking the paradox too literally. Once you know that you are dreaming, it all makes perfect sense. It's actually quite funny. That's the reason you often see the Buddha smiling. He knows the paradox is a drama that we have created in our minds and that really there is only one dreamer: you. The term Buddha means 'Awakened One'. It is a title and does not refer to some God-like figure called Buddha as people so often assume. The truth is that when you know who Buddha is, you realise that he/she is you. But that's probably a little too much for you to take on board at this moment. Perhaps it would best for you to be you and me to be me until we have discussed this dream further.

As you may have gathered, I do not intend to shower you with scientific dogma or philosophical rhetoric in some vain attempt to change your beliefs about your state of consciousness. Instead I would like to take you on a journey through your world to help you to deconstruct and examine your preconceptions in light of the possibility that they may not be based on facts and might instead be embedded in something far more elusive. The conclusions you reach must be your own, of course, but I will act as your guide on this exploratory trip. I have been on many such trips myself, so I am familiar with how the mind reacts when its conception of reality feels threatened.

Don't get me wrong; dreaming is amazing. Who wouldn't want to live in a fantasy where you can have anything you want? But the truth is that, much as we might desire such an existence, it can start to get a little frightening once we begin to take it seriously. In a dream, wherever we go, we end up 'here', because in a dream there is only ever one place and that is wherever you are in the moment. Likewise, no matter what time it is, when you are dreaming it is always 'now'. When space and time, as we know them, start to dissolve into the matrix of the mind, we might start to feel as if we don't actually exist at all and this is when the trip starts to feel bad. We can become overwhelmed if we feel we are freefalling in the eternal abyss of madness and it can feel as though we are losing our purchase on the real world. For some people, this can be too much to handle and they can find themselves suffering from what we term psychosis. Therefore, we have to be careful and prepare ourselves before we take this trip into the nebulous of the dream world.

But let's not too carried away, why don't we just slow down and take a deep breath together. This doesn't have to be a bad trip. Remember that I am your guide and I am here to help you. If, however, our exploration ever does feel too heavy, just take a moment to find your feet and remember these words: 'Everything is exactly as it needs to be. It could be no other way and that is OK. In fact, it's wonderful.' Of course it's wonderful because it's a dream and dreams are made of magic and what could be more fun than that?

Try a Little Magic

I am always careful to distinguish between illusion and magic. One involves fooling someone whereas the other is a far more serious affair. 'Magic' is the term we apply to something that cannot be caught in the net of our everyday language. When we see something we simply cannot explain, we often resort to describing it as magic.

Magic is everywhere. In fact what you are even doing magic at this very moment. Every time you turn the page with your fingers, you make a decision to change it and then you do so. What is peculiar about this decision is that it happens somewhere very unusual: in a place we casually call our mind. But this so-called mind should not be treated so casually. Since the time of the first philosophers, man has wrestled with the problem of the mind. We feel that we 'have' a body but 'are' a mind and that somehow this mind occupies the body. The mind acts as a kind of invisible force that moves the body, but although we can measure the effects of the mind on the body, we have not yet been able to make any measurement of the mind itself.

Neuroscientists have come up with ingenious methods of examining how the brain operates. They can see which parts of the brain become active when we do certain things. In the case of turning the page, a part of the brain called the motor cortex lights up on their imaging devices. This happens when the fingers begin to move. One can say for certain that the motor cortex is involved in movement of the body but this only gives us part of the picture. The part of us that makes the decision to move the hand is nowhere to be found. It's as if the decision just happens, then the motor cortex knows what to do and carries out the prescribed action.

Despite our best efforts to understand the activated brain, we do not yet have any evidence that there is a decision being made anywhere in the brain. It appears to happen all by itself. And yet you or I might argue that we are certain there was a moment when we decided to act, an incident that occurred before we ever turned the page. As far as we are concerned, we could have delayed our decision and made it five minutes later, just to prove a point. By delaying your decision to act, you are showing complete volition over your actions so you can be certain that you have exercised free will and that the decision you made occurred in your own mind, which is, as far as you are concerned, in your head. The fact that scientists can't pinpoint it yet must surely be due to the limitations of their technology, right?

You'd certainly be forgiven for holding such an opinion. After all, isn't that what the world tells you? That you have a body and a mind and that somehow the two interact and that in the future, when our technology is sufficiently advanced, we will be able to draw up mathematical equations of thoughts and design dreams in the same way architects design buildings. This sounds like the kind of description one might find in the pages of scientific texts and fiction alike. However, the brain-mind dilemma is far from solved.

The conventional view of the cosmos is that we are incidental participants in some kind of molecular essay that begin, for no reason, some 13.7 billion years ago. This notion of a material universe suggests that the universe is non-intelligent and that we are simply an accident of chemistry. The fact that we are capable of queering our existential participation in this cosmic operation at all, is all too frequently thrashed and trivialised by a select bunch of self-proclaimed intellectuals, who as it happens, may be completely wrong. Has it ever occurred to you that what is held up as absolute truth does not hold water in your own personal experience? Take your mind, for example. We are told it is in our heads, like some kind of sophisticated machine operator, looking out through our eyes, hearing through our ears and feeling through our skin, but is it really so? Let's test that theory with a little imaginative exercise.

I want you to relax and allow your mind to drift back to a time when you were overjoyed about something in your life. It can be anything, anywhere, as long as you feel like you are present in that moment. I want you to really flood your senses with the memory, to totally immerse yourself in it. Close your eyes and play out the scenario as vividly as possible, seeing what you see, hearing what you hear and feeling what you feel. Then come back to me.

Welcome back. So, did you feel that memory and if so, where? Was it in your head? Perhaps it was your in heart or your tummy or maybe even somewhere deeper, right at the very core of your being, somewhere you can only describe as 'me'. But surely you didn't feel it in your brain. We never actually 'feel' anything in our brains, do we? It is difficult to say where 'you' are; to describe exactly that place you feel and make decisions about turning pages in books. This is really a magical place, which is why we find it so intriguing and, dare I say, even a little paradoxical.

An Experiment in Thinking

Let's try a thought experiment. Thought experiments were used by geniuses like Albert Einstein when he was debating his theories with fellow physicists, so we are adopting a device with great intellectual heritage here.

I want you to imagine that you rubbed your hands together and could both see and feel the rubbing of your hands. According to our current scientific model, there is a part of the brain that moves the hands – this is our motor cortex again – and there is also a part that registers what we see, called the visual cortex. Finally there is a part of the brain that lights up whenever we feel a sensation. This is called the sensory cortex. So the experience of you rubbing your hands together is reflected by the activity of the brain.

Now let's imagine that you were to reach into your head, take out your brain and hold it in your hands for your eyes to see. You are looking at your brain and seeing it with your brain; you are feeling the surface of your brain and feeling it in your brain. How utterly bizarre! Your experience of your brain is being orchestrated by the very thing that you are observing with. You can only ever experience your physical body in your mind and yet you are supposed to believe that the body contains the mind. So which is it: does the body contain the mind or does the mind contain the body?

I think both points of view are right in their own way. It's like when I tell you that you are dreaming; you might agree or disagree depending on your definition of a dream. Dreams are real to the person having the dream in the same way that a story is real to the characters in the book. To the reader, however, there is a kind of dual reality as he/she recognises the realistic intercourse of the various characters, but is nonetheless aware that it is not taking place in the real world. In this regard, we could say that dreams are real when we are in them, but we might describe them more as a pseudo-reality when we wake up and reflect on them retrospectively.

A lucid dreamer has to adopt a very different position when it comes to looking at this as he/she is immersed in the dream reality and possesses, at the same time, a kind of meta-insight into the true nature of his/her experience. He/she can decide what is real and what is not. As Alice said upon her arrival in Wonderland, 'Curiouser and curiouser!' It is very strange indeed to know that you are dreaming while you are dreaming and to feel the full philosophical force of the experience.

The first time I opened my eyes to the world of lucid dreaming, I was enthralled. The idea had been presented to me by a friend – a magical friend, no less. I have practised the art of sleight of hand for many years. I have always been fascinated by how people think and magic tricks give great insight into the nature of the intellect. My friend and I were discussing a trick I like to perform, whereby I have an audience member squeeze a coin in their hand as I hold a cigarette lighter under the palm of my hand and instruct them how they should feel. I introduce metaphors of heating hands and melting chocolate, all the while keeping their focus on the flame. I employ a combination of hypnosis and suggestion and when I ask them to open their hand and reveal the coin they see that it has warped, as if by magic.

I tell them the coin did not bend in their hand but in their mind and that it will only stay bent as long as they believe it is so. As soon as they stop believing in the magic, the coin will flatten out again. I have done this on many occasions and have met numerous people since who still carry the same coin. They tell me that the magic is still with them as the coin remains bent. Some tell me they have shown it to others and told them the story of the coin, so the magic has lived on for many years.

My friend and I both agreed that belief was a very serious topic and it was then that he introduced me to lucid dreaming. He explained that one can become aware of the fact that one is dreaming as long as one believes it is actually possible. This paradox perplexed me. How could one change one's belief about something that was seemingly impossible unless one actually experienced it? Surely it would be impossible to experience something in which one did not believe?

The implications, however, were clear to me. Being able to navigate a dream consciously had to be the gateway to real magic, whatever that was. I had a feeling it had something to do with belief. One thing was certain though: I was destined to find out. A short while later, I had a dream unlike any I had had before. I was dreaming passively one night, as one normally does, until something prompted me to say to myself, 'Hey, I think I'm dreaming.'

That First Dream

I can't say exactly what it was that caused me to realise that I was dreaming that night, but I do remember the subsequent overwhelming urge to interact with the dream environment. And so I defied the laws of gravity by running up a wall and sprinting along its face. It probably lasted for about twenty seconds before I lost my sense of awareness and fell back into the delirium of the dream.

I awoke the next morning both excited and confused. I was unsure whether I had dreamt that I had had a lucid dream or whether I had actually had a lucid dream. The truth is that I just didn't feel I had completely transitioned over the threshold of thought. I had a sense that something was missing. I had to find out what it was. I found the answer to my dilemma when I looked at a website about lucid dreaming for the first time. It listed a variety of techniques to facilitate lucid dreaming, one of which was referred to as a 'reality check'.

A reality check involves testing the nature of the environment one is occupying, to determine whether one is dreaming. It is the reality check, in my view, which separates the semi-lucid from the fully lucid dream. There are as many levels of lucidity as there are levels of awareness in your waking state. It is by no means a simple case of lucid *v.* non-lucid dreaming. There is a whole spectrum of lucidity that begins with realising you are dreaming right up to exhibiting complex dream magic. One can spend many years researching lucid dreaming and still not even scratch the surface.

There are a variety of reality checks that one may use. The first one I attempted was to expect to find a sixth finger on my hand when I thought I might be dreaming. The opportunity to try this came soon after reading about the reality checks online. Again, I don't recall the stimulus. Once more, it occurred to me that I might be dreaming, but this time I was ready to test my environment. I was standing in a shopping mall of the American variety. I knew it was time for my first reality check, so I looked at my left hand, ready to see that extra finger. And there it was, right between my last two fingers. I saw that I had a sixth finger. It looked perfectly natural, as if it were a normal part of my hand. The reality check had worked. I was in!

There are pivotal moments in everyone's life. I don't recall my physical birth, but I do remember that moment of being born into the dream world. It felt like a crucial event after which nothing would ever be the same again. My physical birth delivered me into a finite existence; my second delivered me into infinity. The first thing I did when I realised I was lucid in my dream was to run.

Sheer excitement took over. Then I ran some more. I wasn't trying to go to anywhere in particular. I just ran and ran … I couldn't contain myself, so I just kept on going, trying to see and experience as much as I could. Words cannot express the overwhelming sensation of elation I felt upon realising that I had finally found my way into this limitless world. This was real magic.

What I found most striking was the feeling that my legs were carrying me across the hard floor of the dream; the thud of every footstep, sending shocks up my legs, the kind that one would experience when awake. The ground was solid and it felt real. I found myself racing through a forest with the full force of the breeze in my face. I was surrounded by a variety of familiar vegetation in a typically English forest. Everything was in full bloom. My legs were pumping like pistons, carrying me farther into the magical woodland. 'How incredibly real this is,' I thought to myself.

Then a strange thing happened. The branches reached out, blocking my path. Like some enchanted forest that did not welcome my presence, my passage became so obstructed that I simply had to stop running. I decided to walk down a hill to a little meadow instead. By the time I reached the bottom of the hill, I felt boxed in and wanted desperately to get out and explore some more of this mysterious world. Even though I was in this bizarre dream, I was still able to recall the link for 'Flying Lessons' on the lucid dreaming website. I had specifically decided not to do the lesson as I felt I was not yet at that point, but there I was, feeling like I wanted to fly, but with no instructions on how to do so. I only spent a few seconds thinking about it before I shot up into the air at top speed and flew.

The Insight

I want to draw your attention to the terrific insight I had in the dream. I was able to recall the website and my use of it. I was able to consider my dilemma clearly. This is the kind of mental negotiation we would not normally associate with dreaming. It is a demonstration of the degree of consciousness possible in a lucid dream. The dream continued for about ten minutes, at the end of which I awoke amazed, not just at the fact that I had joined this exclusive club of lucid dreamers, but also at just how real it had seemed to me. I knew that I had stumbled across something significant, something that could change the world for all of us.

Performing a reality check made the experience all the more real as it gave me the certainty that had been lacking in my previous lucid dream. A reality check tends to work very well. I say 'tends to' because there is always a chance of failure, even if you know are dreaming. The reason for this is belief or lack of belief. If one does not believe in one's attempt to perform a reality check, it may not work. This is an important concern as the implications are far-reaching.

A common reality check is to try to stick one's finger through the palm of one's hand. This is an exceptionally effective reality check. Most lucid dreamers have tried it. The most interesting thing about this is that we all tend to get slightly different results. In some cases the finger goes right through the hand; in others, the skin stretches over the intruding finger, like a tent being pitched; and, in other cases, the finger does not go through the hand at all. There is no strict set of outcomes, the likes of which might infer an underlying rule system. Instead we are looking at something much more unfamiliar to our model of reality, something lacking precise rules.

Another common reality check is to try to pull one's index finger, stretching it like an elastic digit. I have achieved it on a number of occasions but it is not always possible. Neither, for example, is flying. Sometimes it's easy to fly, but sometimes it's more of a challenge. A common reality check is to lean forwards to see if one can float; if the body feels light enough, one can let oneself drift off the floor to confirm that one is dreaming. The late

Bill Hicks used to tell a joke about the LSD user who jumped off a building and, in the process, messed it up for the rest of us by giving LSD a bad name. Bill suggests that he should have tried a test flight first by jumping into the air rather than just plummeting to his death. In the case of the suggested reality check, I too recommend a test flight before trying anything more extravagant.

A safer reality check involves pinching the nose, then attempting to breathe in through one's nose. This is a reliable reality check. It hasn't failed me yet. A more dubious reality check, on the other hand, is to ask oneself if one remembers how one got here as dreams will rarely oblige you with any kind of memory. So one might consider this a kind of reality check, but of course the fact that you don't remember how you got to the top of a building is not an invitation to jump off. Use your judgement at all times and just think about what Bill Hicks would have said, 'Don't screw it up for the rest of us!'

Reading text, then looking away and back again is a good method of determining whether or not you are dreaming. The likelihood is that the text will be very difficult to read in the first place, if it's readable at all, and the second viewing will invariably yield something different to what you first saw. Digital clocks also seem to suffer from the same lack of continuity, as do the palms of your hands. Just look at them, turn them over and repeat the process of investigating them. You will probably find that they seem different. In some cases, they can appear to be quite strange-looking. My friend, the lucid dream expert, Robert Waggoner, tells a great story in his book *Lucid Dreaming – Gateway to the Inner Self* about how he used to look for his hands in his dreams in order to become lucid. His first lucid dream was triggered by his hands being randomly propelled up into his face. The subsequent realisation took him on the first of many wild adventures.

Reality checks are a great way to test both the quality of the environment and to assess your own awareness. Naturally, there will be times when you are more experienced when you will simply know that you are in the dream state and performing a reality check will seem superfluous. But it is a good habit to perform a reality check anyway, just in case you are wrong. This was the attitude I adopted from the beginning, but what I found particularly troubling was the fact that sometimes, even when I knew I was dreaming, I couldn't get the reality checks to work 100 per cent of the time. My attitude has always been that if it is my dream and I know I am dreaming, then surely the reality checks should be successful, but strangely that hasn't always been the case.

This got me thinking a lot about the nature of belief. What is belief and how do we alter it? Is it a trivial part of our psyche or is it more significant than that? These questions are not easily answered, but as we venture deeper down the rabbit hole of consciousness, they will have a far greater role to play in understanding how it is that we experience our world. When dreaming, you intuit that belief is likely to have an influence on events. After all, isn't that what are dreams made of?

Let me frame this little for you. Consider any object you see in the room around you, even the book you are holding right now. Our current scientific model tells us this book is made of atoms, which in turn are made of electrons, protons, neutrons and so forth. Imagine that the book in your hands is a dream book and that you are actually in a dream. What is the dream book composed of now? Could it, too, be made of atoms? If so, might we suggest that dreams, by implication, are also made of atoms and moreover, what could this possibly tell us about the true nature of reality?

2) Evolving Times

Some years ago I was snowboarding in France and ended up in hospital with a broken leg. I needed a little help with the pain as the break was severe. A couple of days later, dosed up on some analgesics, I joked to my identical twin, who was visiting me at the time, that I remembered a character from history by the name of Ignatius Loyola, who had a mystical vision after having his leg blown off by a cannon ball. The Spaniard had a religious awakening and subsequently proceeded to form an outfit known as the Jesuits, who went on to spread the message of Christianity as an army of warrior priests. I jested that I too might have such an insight here in my debilitated state.

Later that night I couldn't sleep as my roommate was snoring. Tossing and turning was not an option as my leg was tied up, so I grew frustrated. I decided to try to meditate. I figured that some deep relaxation might help, as it had done many times before. It did the trick and I got to sleep. However, the cocktail of medication, pain, snoring, tiredness and deep relaxation sent me into an unfamiliar state of consciousness; I became vaguely aware of the fact that I was dreaming.

I found myself wandering through London's Hyde Park, walking along a familiar-looking path on my way to meet someone who was waiting for me. I was occasionally mildly lucid, but I could not control the experience. I simply watched through the eyes of the dreamer as a waking observer. Finally I got to the end of the path. The person waiting for me was upright and staunch, neutral-faced but with an air of friendliness and familiarity. There was no denying who it was that awaited me – it was my own self.

By now, I had more of a firm grip on my reality. I was awake in my hospital bed and staring around the half-lit dawn drenched room. I cleared my throat and coughed a few times in an attempt to wake my French torturer from his insulting slumber. In my half-conscious weariness it occurred to me that I might still be dreaming.

Within a few seconds, the room grew so bright it hurt my eyes. As I wiped them, I knew I was back in familiar territory, it was late morning and I was firmly tied up in my hospital bed, curious and confused and desperate to ask one of the nurses if I was still dreaming or not. At the risk of being dragged from the recovery room to the psychiatric ward, I did not stir and put the experience down to my altered chemistry but I was smitten by the blurring of reality and my inner world, which had felt so real.

I eventually discovered that what I had experienced is known as a false awakening, which is when one wakes from a dream into another dream, normally in the room in which one is sleeping. This is a strange experience because one is convinced one is awake. What has actually transpired usually only becomes apparent to the dreamer upon waking in their actual place of sleep. It is possible to experience a number of false awakenings in a row. Robert Waggoner tells a story about how he once had several false awakenings, each one making him feel progressively more concerned as he was lucidly aware of his unfolding circumstances. He eventually resigned himself to whatever he awakened to and was ready accept it, no matter absurd it might have been. He did arrive safely back in his bedroom and survived to tell the tale in his lectures on the subject.

The Hammer Test

The ambiguity that we encounter in our reality in altered states of consciousness suggests that the world may actually be regarded as a state of mind rather than something solid and 'real'. There is a saying in the scientific community, 'If you can hit it with a hammer, then it is real and if not, then it isn't.' I always get a laugh out this. If we accept that the world is material and that mind and emotion are simply expressions of physical phenomena, then I guess it's possible to hit my laughter on the head, but that doesn't make a whole lot of sense, does it?

This is the physiological conundrum we are faced with in today's world. How can something material, like my brain, give rise to something immaterial, like my love of Turkish delight or the beauty of a sunset or something tragic like the loss of a loved one? To be human is to be greater than the sum of our parts, to be more than just a biological hard drive that pushes us about the planet. We are the inheritors of something unique. It is, as far as we can tell, the most advanced technology in the universe. I am, of course, talking about the imagination.

As a lucid dreamer, I know that I have a unique perspective, not just on my dreams, but also on the nature of reality itself. Until now, we have modelled the human mind by observing behaviour processes and marrying them to the neurological patterns of electrical activity in our brain systems. Not a bad start, but hardly a conclusive position, especially when we take lucid dreaming and all of its implications into account. If we are to adopt the position of the lucid explorer, what we are offered is a first-hand investigation of the dream world. Lucid dreamers are the frontiersmen of a new landscape. The stories we return with may seem outlandish but they are at least relevant to our view of reality. One might even go so far as to say that lucid dreaming is crucial because it allows us to peer into the abyss of our own minds.

However, despite the incredible view of reality that lucid dreaming offers us, the world of conventional science has been slow on the uptake. The practice of lucid dreaming has existed for thousands of years but, to the Western World, it has always been thought of as akin to scientific fiction. But, as I often tell people, today's science fiction is tomorrow's scientific fact.

We live in a world of proof and the scientific evidence needed to qualify lucid dreaming was finally provided by two independent researchers over four decades ago. Both teams contrived the same experiment to demonstrate the possibility of a dreamer becoming aware of their hybrid state of consciousness. This involved having the dreamer communicate their state of consciousness back to an independent observer under lab-tested conditions. American scientist Dr Steven LaBerge and Englishman Dr Keith Hearne are the two men responsible for this famous experiment. It is LaBerge who is normally given credit; however, I think it is only fair to say that both men empirically proved the possibility of lucid dreaming and thus made the first step towards a new set of rules for the way we investigate dreaming today.

The experiment (in both cases) was based on a predetermined sequence of eye movements. These were prepared with a clinical team, prior to the subject sleeping. The agreed movements would act as a signal that the dreamer had become lucid in his or her dream. So, for example, moving the eyes to the left, then to the right, six times was the signal that the dreamer had become lucid. To prove that one is dreaming, one would have to be asleep, of course, so a device called an electric encephalograph (EEG) was used to monitor brainwave activity. During the REM stage of sleep, the sleeper is most likely to be dreaming. This can be indicated by the EEG.

During this stage, we would expect the person to be unable to move as most of the body is physically paralyzed by natural blockage of electrical impulses from the brain to the spinal cord during sleep. This is nature's way of preventing us from carrying out our dreams. Our involuntary muscles (lungs, heart, etc.) still function normally. Another set of muscles that remain active are those that move the eyes. As we do not ordinarily feel movement of the eyes under our lids, there is no likely feedback mechanism that could cause us to wake up and disturb the dreaming process, so we can sleep, paralyzed but stable, and the research team can take advantage of this eye movement.

The eyes frequently move rapidly during sleep, especially during the REM period, but they can also occasionally mimic the movement of the eyes of the dreaming subject. In the case of a lucid dream if, for example, we look left in a dream then our physical eyes do likewise. In LaBerge's and Hearne's lab tests, an electroocculograph (EOG) was employed to detect retinal movement. When dreaming started, the pre-arranged eye movements were made by the lucid dreamer to affirm that he (LaBerge was his own subject and Hearne used a man named Alan Worsley) was aware that he was dreaming. This was one of the greatest breakthroughs ever made in dream science; a dreaming subject was communicating to the waking world that he knew he was dreaming.

However when LaBerge first presented his findings to the prestigious magazine *Science*, his work was rejected. Likewise the British magazine *Nature* returned his paper without review. The editors did not think lucid dreaming was of 'sufficient interest' to merit consideration.

This is indicative of a deep cultural prejudice as to what defines 'reality' within the scientific community, one I will address in more detail a little later. For now, all I will say is that the climate is changing, thankfully. With the advent of the internet, we are moving away from a communication system of 'one to many' to a 'many to many' design. This means that we are no longer at the whim of a single person's opinion on how the world works, but instead are entering into full and open discussion with each other.

A Plasticity of Fact

Historically, we lived in a world of so-called facts, which were really no more than cultural notions neatly gathered up between the hard covers of books and passed on from one misinformed generation to the next. The conclusions drawn from these facts were spoon-fed to us by those who found themselves in the fortunate position of being in charge of how we think. This, in turn, led to a great deal of problems as populations were poisoned by crude politics and delusions of a quasi-religious nature. But Mother Nature is not mute and she did what she does best by connecting us in ways we have never experienced before.

It is my opinion that two of the most important events in human history are the birth of language and the advent of the internet. Both are expressions of the same basic process: communication, or the transfer of information. Language is what connected us in the first place, but it also eventually divided us. Nowadays the globalisation of the planet through fibre-optic technology is changing the way we speak to each other. It no longer matters whether you are part of the elite hierarchy or not. Anyone can have a voice.

We are no longer living in a world in which reality is prescribed to us by those who claim to know better. This is true people power, we are destabilising the system by rewriting the rules with social networking. Anyone can have an idea and if enough people like it, it can gain momentum and become something more. Take, for example, crowdfunding – somebody takes something from their imagination and holds it up to the world. If there is enough interest, the product can be developed thanks to financial support from the online community and so imagination becomes reality in the most literal way.

When I suggest to someone that they are dreaming, they immediately assume I am implying that they are asleep somewhere else. But when have we ever experienced a dream with our eyes closed? One could argue that when we are dreaming, there is the implication that our physical eyes are closed and our bodies are resting, but for the dreamer, this is not the case. The dreaming individual only ever experiences his or her reality as you and I are doing right now, with our eyes wide open.

Dreaming is not about having your eyes closed. On the contrary, it is about opening your eyes to the nature of your world. This is precisely what lucid dreaming proposes. It is an insight into the true state of your being. This is the attitude I adopt when I think about reality. How can we define our world when information itself has become so plastic? Facts have dissolved into special effects on videos and contested notions on Wikipedia. How can we say what is real anymore?

There was a great deal of talk about the end of the world in 2012 and yet we all woke up this morning to a world that was still here. But the world, as we knew it, did end sometime in the last twenty years or so. The very thing that held our world together – the fact – went into decline, leaving the future of what we once called the truth on rocky ground.

The world we are living in today is very much a product of whatever websites you decide to visit. Take 9/11. What really happened and who did it? Was it a terrorist attack or a cynical act of the American state, designed to stir up trouble with its neighbours in the east? Or could it have been caused by a UFO? It all depends on who you are willing to believe and what sites you visit to verify your facts. There are plenty of people out there willing to show you their proof, which is often surprisingly compelling.

I only invoke this example to draw attention to the new ways of examining our world, which do not rely exclusively on the ideas of others. We must look beyond the boundaries of convention to re-empower our own personal experience.

This would involve an intellectual departure from the contrived notions of others towards the world as we experience it in our own minds. In light of this, lucid dreaming may take on a very important role. In the world of the dream, your personal experience is all there is. An investigation of this can provide some interesting answers about the human psyche and perhaps even more.

Self-Experimentation

As a lucid dreamer, I am well aware of the need to practise self-experimentation. This has a great scientific heritage, although it is frequently frowned upon nowadays. This is largely because of the ethical concerns: that one might cause harm to one's self or that there might be too subjective an outcome to offer any verifiable data. I understand these concerns but I ask that the reader consider that what we are discussing here is a shift in the nature of enquiry. Self-experimentation, although potentially dangerous, is critical for the lucid dreamer, as he or she is usually the only audience to this very personal experience.

I was wary of the danger of self-harm, but in the spirit of exploration I was willing to put myself on the line. I have always been inspired by great explorers, men who walked on the moon or traversed impossible landscapes in pursuit of a higher truth. I recall the story of an Australian physician, the Nobel Prize winner Professor Barry Marshall, who controversially inoculated himself with bacteria in an effort to reverse decades of medical doctrine by showing that peptic ulcers were, in fact, caused by *Helicobacter pylori* – a micro-organism, and not by stress and too much acidic food, as had previously been assumed.

One night, having become lucid in a dream, I decided to try out the hammer test (hitting something with a hammer to prove it is solid, even if it is a 'dream solid'). Having found the equivalent of a hammer – it was actually a dream book I found – I decided the target would be none other than my own finger.

Faced with the genuine threat of pain, I did not want to choose one of my own five fingers, so instead I performed a reality check. I looked away from my hand and expected to see a sixth finger on my left hand when I looked at it again. It had worked before and it might have worked this time, but it did not alas, so I had to use one of my own fingers. I chose my pinkie and laid it out on a dream table, which felt perfectly solid. I adopted a conservative strategy and decided to tap my finger with the book end. It made a familiar sound and felt right, even if it was a little soft. The myth about not being able to feel pain in dreams, from which we get the 'pinch' test, does not hold water. Although we do not ordinarily feel pain in dreams, it is possible and in some cases, as with post-traumatic stress disorder (PTSD), the person can feel full and even amplified sensations of pain as they relive the trauma.

So it is possible to feel something solid and even painful in a dream, but I wondered what the implications of this were? Did it mean my familiar world of atoms and molecules was coming undone at the seams? That is how it felt at the time. How could I look at things the same way again? The dream world was proving to be as vast, complex and even tangible as the physical world. What I once defined as reality was quickly losing traction in my mind and dreaming was taking on a new role.

My experiments would soon progress to more daring and outlandish essays in self-discovery. I would eventually raise the bar to terrifying new heights. But before we move on to this, we need to spend some time with the atom. If we are to make the daring suggestion that dreams are made of something equivalent to matter, we need to address what is referred to as tautology. Tautology is a logical argument that ends up repeating the same concept or phraseology to no real end.

When I tell someone about my hammer test in the dream, they are quick to point out that my experience was exactly what I expected it would be because dreaming is forged by both memory and expectation. I can see how such an argument might feel complete to someone who had not considered the matter adequately. Expectation and memory can influence the outcome of the experience, though this is not always the case, as we will soon see, but that hardly is tantamount to defining the nature of the experience itself. It does not even begin to tell us what dreams are actually made of. Surely we can't say they are made of expectations or memories as we have no definitions for these either. Some people tell me that dreams are made of thoughts. When I reply, by asking, 'In that case, might we ask what are thoughts made of?' I am often subjected to some flustered response about brains and electrical signalling, but that tells me nothing about my finger being pounded with a book end. To say that dreams occur in your head is an inadequate position as no one has ever witnessed a dream in a head. No one has ever seen a thought in a head either. The most we can say about thoughts is that they are made of whatever we think they are made of, which is tragically tautological.

The 'Q' Word

Our dilemma should be apparent. We, the observers, are entangled in the outcome of our own observation, making it impossible to talk about matters in an objective manner. This is anathema to the scientific community. Physicists happily boast of their ability to observe scientific processes in completely isolated conditions, as in a vacuum, while we lucid dreamers are hopelessly tied up in the outcome of our own experiments. However, as I hope to show you, when we probe a little deeper into the world of modern science, we will find that it is less objective than many of its practitioners would like to admit.

This subject is riddled with rhetoric and it is too often misused by pseudo-spiritual types to conceal a lack of any real knowledge. I will do my best to weave together both my experience of lucid dreaming and my understanding of quantum physics to form a palatable and digestible serving of meaningful information. Now that the 'Q' word has been used, we can ask what all the fuss is about and why it has turned the world of science upside down. Does the advent of quantum physics herald a genuine change in how we can actually appraise our world?

I like to approach science not as a destination but as a kind of road sign. As such, I will not offer the quantum mechanical view as a conclusion on how we should understand the nature of our world, but instead I will ask you to see it as a reflection of what is taking place in our consciousness. The quantum view has not only revolutionised our understanding of matter; it has paved the way for a new kind of language, which may eventually resolve the paradox in our reality. But this won't come easy. To quote the brilliant physicist Niels Bohr, 'If quantum physics hasn't profoundly shocked you, you haven't understood it yet.'

When we discuss the physical world, we usually talk about the properties of matter according to size. Anything smaller than an atom is on the sub-atomic scale, this is where quantum mechanics come into play. Matter on a larger scale obeys the laws of classic or Newtonian physics. The latter term refers to mass and gravity, as defined by Newton's laws and Einstein's theories of special and general relativity. Without going into explicit detail, these ideas are not only experimentally verifiable and mathematically complete in their own right; they also marry with our experience of everyday reality. Quantum mechanics, on the other hand, does not.

Time and space are the bookends of our world. In between, objects move according to their mass and momentum. It is all predictable. One could be forgiven for assuming that the world of science has arrived at a complete theory of everything. However, when we open up the atom, we see that matters can be very different indeed. Quantum physics has turned our view of reality on its head, not so much because it is difficult to understand but more because it is difficult to accept.

Nobel Prize winner Richard Feynman, considered by many to be one of the foremost advocates of the quantum view of reality, famously expressed his opinion that the mystery of quantum physics was to be found in one single experiment, 'the double-slit experiment'. I like to describe this experiment by priming audiences with another thought experiment. I want you to imagine you are standing in your bedroom, having just realised that you are dreaming. Before you leave your room to go on a lucid adventure, would you say that the rest of your house is already there or is it only going to be there when you observe it?

Dreaming Up a New Model

If we adopt the position that dreams are made of thoughts, then, as we only ever experience thoughts in the moment they arise, it follows that that the dimensions of the dream would be limited to our immediate observations. The bedroom you see around you would be all that your mind is processing. The mind would not have created the rest of your house yet for if it had, one might as well assume that it had also created the surrounding streets and houses, street lights, cars, traffic lights, people and places, extending outwards to infinity, which sounds dubious.

My feeling is that what you are experiencing in a dream is the boundary of your reality. When you leave your dream bedroom, it is likely that the next room will not mirror the architecture of your home perfectly because dreams, as we know, are not subject to the same rigorous rules of space and time as the physical world. In dreams, people, places and possibilities all get mixed up and we can therefore enter into just about any kind of arena. This implies that there is no fixed world outside of your dream bedroom before you actually leave it.

With this in mind, I propose a model of reality consisting of three layers. The first layer is that which we can observe directly. In the case of the above lucid dream, this would be your bedroom. The second is that which is implied by what we know about the circumstances, but cannot be observed directly. In the dream, this would be the rest of your house, which you know to hold your bedroom. We can't see it directly but we accept that it should be there. The third layer is that which cannot be observed and can only be very loosely assumed to exist. In the dream, this would be the country in which your house is located, the planet, the solar system, the galaxy and so on.

If we examine the dream world and assume it is being constructed by the mind alone, we might feel more comfortable adopting the view that it is only the first, or surface, layer of reality that is being generated and that the other two layers do not exist at all. This might seem more plausible to us than the idea that our brains have the capacity to create the entire universe every night. I might direct the reader's attention back to my previous proposal that creation and experience are concurrent events in dreams; in other words, what you see is what you get and there is no more.

Let's take our thought experiment back to the physical world and consider a flower. We have only discovered in recent years that bees have the ability to see light in the ultraviolet range, which is not possible for the human eye. So what we see and what the bee sees are different versions of the same thing. Thus, the outer layer of reality, as we have defined it, cannot be considered an objective event as it is affected by the species observing it.

The physicist will usually argue that this is only a surface-level concern as the implied reality, or second layer, is unaffected by the observer, which is to say that regardless of whether it is a bee or a human that is looking, there is still a fixed, objective aspect to the flower that precipitates what we see on the outer surface of reality and so, even though it may vary its external appearance, there is still an actual flower there. As I have already discussed, I do not expect this to be the case for a dream flower. In the dream world, the first layer will always be subjective to the observer and, by proxy, so will the second layer. The entire dream will be subjective, so we cannot talk about an objective undertone, but the jury is still out on the physical world. Does science stand on solid foundations? Is there a verifiably objective layer we can drill down to?

The building blocks that make up our world – protons, neutrons, electrons, quarks etc. – may not behave as obediently as we have formerly been led to believe by the scientific community. The truth is that the second layer of reality may be violated by the

39

enigma that has had the world of science up in arms for over 100 years, 'the double-slit experiment'.

The experiment is easier to understand if one is willing to be flexible in one's conception of reality so let's try. Imagine a gun that shoots tiny ball bearings, in a randomly scattering fashion, at a metal screen which is ordinarily impenetrable to the bearings but does, however, have a narrow slit in the middle which allows some bearings to pass through. Those that pass through hit a detector screen on the other side. This screen acts like shooting target marking paper as it gives us an indication of where the bearings hit.

What we would expect to see after a brief period of time would be marks on the target, a vertical line made up of little dots, each one representing the successful passage of a bearing through the slit. As we are shooting randomly at the slit, we can expect that all of the ball bearings will enter and hence exit the slot at different angles. This causes an accumulation of hits, which would be at their densest directly opposite the slit and would fade out on either side until there is no marking at all (see Figure 1).

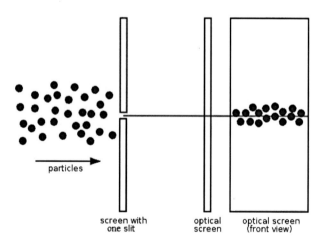

Figure 1

Let's imagine a similar experiment; this time with two slits rather than one (see Figure 2). You might be able to deduce from our first result how this is experiment would turn out – two vertical bands of positive activity (hits), each one with the highest area of density in the centre opposite the slit, with action fading out on either side.

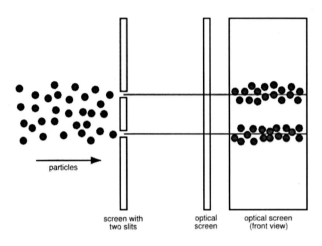

screen with   optical   optical screen
two slits   screen   (front view)

particles

Figure 2

We are now going to introduce a new medium to measure. We will continue to use our metal shield with a single slit, only this time we will pass water through the screen. We will also substitute the target board with a special detector screen so we can measure how the water behaves as it passes through the slit. Water moves in waves. These waves consist of high points known as peaks and low points known as troughs. In our single-slit experiment, the water hits the slit and a wave emerges on the opposite side. It hits the detector screen with maximum intensity right in the centre because this is where the peak of the wave is. The activation of the detector screen fades off gradually on either side towards the troughs, which leave no mark at all. So our results looks very similar to those we saw earlier with the ball bearings – a vertical band of activity directly opposite the slit, fading out gradually on either side but the wave spreads out much further (see Figure 3). *The illustrations below are substituting water with a monochromatic laser as this will illustrate the same effect.*

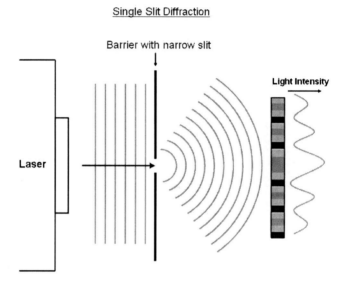

Figure 3

When the water (or laser wave) travels instead through two slits, it emerges as two waves, which spread out and interact with each other before hitting the detector screen. The pattern that emerges is what we call an interference pattern, which occurs because of the way the peaks and troughs of the waves interact. When two peaks meet, they amplify each other to make an even bigger wave (the sum of the two peaks). When a peak and trough meet, they cancel each other out, neutralising the form. When the water/laser hits our screen, we end up with a series of bands. The heaviest band is found in middle, between the two slits. Both above and below this are bands of neutral detection, which are followed in turn by progressively lighter bands, each one interrupted by an area of zero impact (see Figure 4).

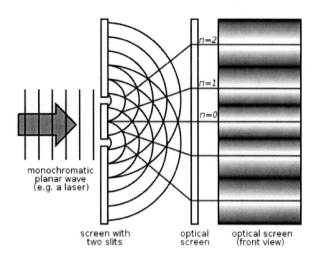

Figure 4

So far we have shot solid matter and waves of material through our slits. We can describe a piece of solid matter, like one of our ball bearings, as a particle. This distinguishes it from matter in a more flowable form, like the waves of water. These terms (particle and wave) are important.

We are now going to shift the scale of our scientific apparatus down to the quantum level of activity by using a gun that shoots tiny pieces of matter called electrons. These are very much like our ball bearings, in that they can be treated as particles and they too mark the detector screen with a single vertical band when they are shot randomly through a single slit. But when we shoot them through the double slit arrangement, we do not get the anticipated two vertical bands that one would expect with particles. What we get is an interference pattern. (See Figure 5)

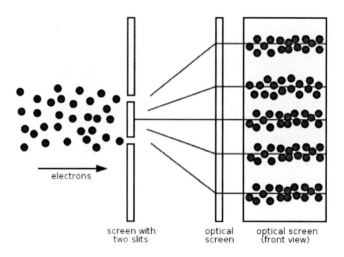

electrons

screen with   optical   optical screen
two slits   screen   (front view)

Figure 5

This result points to the very heart of quantum physics. Understanding it is the key to opening your mind to a new way of thinking about the nature of reality. In summary, when we measure the behaviour of what we would normally conceive of as a solid piece of matter at the sub-atomic scale, it behaves in a wave-like fashion. To put it another way, something we would normally consider to be very precise and rigid acts as if it were an indistinct, flowable form.

What we will discover when we fine-tune our understanding of this will force us to seriously reconsider the question I proposed in the last chapter: could dreams be made of atoms and, if so, could the property of quantum matter revealed by the last experiment give us some idea of how this might actually be possible?

3) Tangled Thoughts

Like Alice tumbling down the rabbit hole, we can begin to ponder the implications of this new paradigm. Until now the building blocks of our world were tiny bits of matter known as particles. These blocks were, in turn, cemented together by wave-like energies, such as water or electromagnetic radiation. These bookends of our world were understood in such a way that the world seemed like a rather pragmatic and predictable place in which to live.

Eventually we determined that separating the building blocks and looking at them individually might give us further insight into the nature of our world. It was not long before we had an arsenal of instruments with which we could examine the atom. But that had its own tautological implications. How could we look inside of an atom and not end up in a kind of hall of mirrors?

The idea of an objective world is hardly a naïve notion. It is born of our experience of how the world feels to us; most of us feel as though we have arrived in this world, which existed before we did and will be here after we are gone. We feel immersed in a system that eventually grinds us out of existence, a process that is facilitated by space and time.

The mechanics of space and time have been well documented by the scientific community. Rules governing how things work have been carefully discerned through mathematical hypotheses and validated by rigorous experimentation. Our sophisticated understanding of the nature of things has allowed us to create, for example, a portable device with which one can find virtually any fact or fiction recorded by humans. It seems inconceivable and yet it is true.

The boundaries of epistemology are finally being breached as we push aside the printing press and make way for a new kind of information system. We no longer look for truth in outdated ideologies, which threaten eternal damnation for those who question their truth. Instead, we seek meaning by embracing personal experience. After centuries of exile we, the people, are once more acting of our own accord.

But our experiments with ball bearings, water and electrons have shaken the foundations of this reality ...

A Little Interference

The experiment consisted of shooting matter through a metal plate via one or two slits. On a screen on the other side, we would expect to see certain patterns emerging, depending on the type of matter (particles or waves) and how many slits used. The particles would tend to leave vertical bands of hits, opposite the slits, and the waves, when passed through the double-slit apparatus, would leave a more complex series of bands, separated by intervals of zero impact. This is the classic interference pattern. We can say that, at the macro level of everyday physics, the outcome is consistent to such a degree that we could almost call it a rule.

However, things became more complicated when we used sub-atomic matter. We discovered that electrons, when fired at the double-slit screen and left for a little while, would eventually create an interference pattern which, as far as we knew, was impossible – unless the laws of physics for the sub-atomic world are different from those which apply to the bigger world.

But scientists weren't convinced. They thought that perhaps these little particles were hitting off each other, causing a bouncing effect, which in turn created the wave-like interference pattern.

It seemed like a plausible suggestion. In order to investigate, they slowed down the rate at which the particles were fired and shot them one at a time. This would eliminate the possibility of the particles bumping off each other and would almost certainly stop this interference silliness, wouldn't it?

After an hour or two of testing, physicists were surprised to find not the two vertical bands they had predicted but rather the same interference pattern again. The conclusion was certain. The electron was leaving the gun as a particle, assuming the properties of a wave, entering both slits and leaving as two more waves (as a wave would). These two waves, in turn, would interact with each other and hit the detector to create the interference pattern on the detection screen, but how?

They decided to repeat the experiment, this time recording and monitoring the electrons as they passed from the gun through the slits to determine which slit the particle went through and how this occurred. The result came as a shock.

While the electrons were being observed, they assumed the properties of the particle – that is to say, they went through either of the two slits individually and marked the detector screen with a gradual accumulation of two vertical bands opposite the slits. The very act of observation changed the behaviour of the electrons so they assumed the properties of particles rather than waves. It seemed impossible, or at least highly implausible. How could matter have any reaction to our looking at it? Was it somehow aware of our presence?

This is one of the most controversial discoveries in the history of physics. It is relevant to all known matter, including light, which we discovered can also act as particle-like pieces, known as photons. Time and time again, experimental data has confirmed that matter, when we try to reduce it to its properties, can exhibit either wave- or particle-like behaviour, depending on whether or not we observe it. When we are monitoring it, matter exhibits orderly, particle-like behaviour and when left to its own devices, it exhibits wave-like behaviour.

At this time, I would like to remind you of what we set out to achieve. I proposed that our species is experiencing a shift of consciousness, which is being ushered in by the internet. It is online that new paradigms and possibilities are being discussed without restriction. People are sharing their personal experiences of altered states of consciousness. We are paving the way for a new model of reality by marrying our own anecdotal experiences with essays on physics. We should not, however, make wild assumptions about the nature of the cosmos; instead, we should try to elaborate appropriately on what the physicists are telling us about their understanding of matter. We will link this back to lucid dreaming later as I want to keep your attention focussed solely on the physics for now.

If you want to see the hair stand up on the back of a physicist's neck, just mention the 'measurement problem'. This arises when we try to describe the essence of a piece of matter. To say that it is either a wave or a particle is technically incorrect for we discover that when we are forced to measure it the world of matter starts to act strangely. In order to understand this conundrum, we have to turn to the abstract world of pure mathematics.

We now adopt the expression 'wave property' and describe it not as an actual wave but instead as a mathematical apparatus, the likes of which we use in statistical analyses. This is also known as a distribution curve. It is typically expressed as a wave-shaped graph that pits two aspects of something against each other. In the case of the electron, we chart the position against the probability of finding it somewhere. The peak of the wave tells us where we are most likely to find the electron the most number of times (the highest probability). On either side of this point, the distribution curve gradually decreases in both directions simultaneously until there is no possibility of finding it anywhere anymore (see Figure 1).

Quantum Wave Function

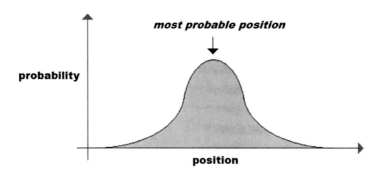

Figure 1

The figure describes the likelihood of finding a particle in any given place at any given time. We call this the quantum wave function. This is not the same thing as saying the particle is anywhere prior to our taking a measurement, nor is it suggesting that the particle is spread across all possible locations until we actually observe it. It is a purely hypothetical apparatus and does not speculate about where the particle might be prior to measurement; only that it exists in a kind of mathematical super-position until we take a measurement. *There is no electron at this stage. We are considering it purely as a potential event, but we cannot say where or when it will take place yet.*

The act of observing satisfies the *when*, as our measurement causes the wave function to collapse from a super state (all possibilities) into a single determined state. This is what we saw with our double-slit experiment. Prior to our observation, matter behaved like a wave function, which passed through two slits and exited as two more wave functions that interfered with each other, giving rise to the classic interference pattern on the detector screen. By contrast, when we used cameras to observe the electrons, two vertical bands appeared on the screen, indicating particle behaviour. This, we infer, occurred because our observation caused the wave function to collapse prior to entering the slits and so precipitated the particle into a tangible existence. Thus it was a particle that passed through the slit and not a wave function.

What we have here is a mathematical condition which, when perturbed by our conscious interaction, precipitates the physical properties of the electrons. It would seem that one had plucked something out of thin air, as if by magic. Perhaps even more interesting is the fact that the two components of the mathematical abstraction, our hypothetical wave patterns, are able to interact with each other in a manner we would normally only ever associate with physical waves. The interference pattern we end up with in the 'unobserved' set-up of the experiment implies that matter behaves like a real wave and marks the screen in the same way, but when we try to observe these weird waves they immediately start acting as particles, so we never get to see them as waves. This is why we must infer their presence and only ever refer to them indirectly, in mathematical terms.

We might take a moment to revisit our description of reality as consisting of three layers. We stated that the outermost layer is visible to us and the second layer implies this. We also said that in dreaming we were willing to consider the outer layer as the primary experience and were even willing to more or less dismiss the other two layers. Thanks to our experiment, we are able to offer some credence to the second layer because there is where the waves allegedly interfere with each other.

Remember, however, that we do not witness this directly. As soon as we observe the wave activity, it behaves in a particle-like manner. By bringing this second layer of activity to the surface, we cause it to change its behaviour and crystallise into something tangible. Perhaps we could say the same of dreaming, in that we can have many thoughts, interfering with and informing each other, prior to their manifestation in a dream, at which point they become the tangible landscape of our experience.

Heisenberg's Uncertainty

We must now ask ourselves whether the term 'either/or' is a
satisfactory intellectual position to assume. How can we talk of
matter as not being one thing or another and yet somehow being
both at the same time? The person who formulated the most potent
mathematical picture of this strange behaviour was a theoretical
physicist by the name of Werner Heisenberg. The German Nobel
Prize winner made a ground-breaking contribution to modern
physics and is regarded as one of the founders of quantum
mechanics. His theory, known as the *uncertainty principle*, was first
published in 1927. It is still sending shockwaves through the minds
of physicists today because its implications reach right to the heart
and soul of matter: the wave/particle problem.

We have established two different outcomes to our experiment,
which are determined by the introduction or removal of
surveillance technology, so it is here that we need to focus our
attention. In the experiment in which we openly observe the
electrons, they assume particle-like behaviour throughout the
process. That is to say, they act consistently from start to finish.
In the 'unobserved' experiment, we leave it for a while before
we check the results, which demonstrate that the electrons have
behaved in a wave-like manner. If we open up a viewing gallery to
see what is going on during the experiment, then we get particle-
like behaviour again. Scientists thought that perhaps covering
up and subsequently unveiling the experiment introduced light
into the equation, which could be responsible for the changed
behaviour. They came up with a compelling argument, one which
people often invoke, but does it really hold water?

Light is a form of matter. Although there is much debate about
whether light has mass, we know that it does have energy and
momentum. It was proposed that the act of observation in our
experiment introduced light photons into our apparatus, which
could somehow displace the electrons, causing them to act in a

particle-like fashion. It was proposed that this might explain why waves sometimes behave like particles. Scientists concluded that if this were the case, the strange results would be merely a reflection of the limitations of our technology.

The dilemma is often referred to as the observer effect. When one first encounters the light explanation, one might feel relieved that the world is returning to some kind of normality. But there is yet another twist to the tale ...

Heisenberg was unperturbed by the assumption that light was the cause of the changed behaviour of the electrons. He went on to prove that what we were witnessing was far more alarming. He asserted that there was a certain fundamental limit to the precision with which certain pairs of physical properties of matter could be known. These values are known as *complementary variables* and they are a reflection of the wave/particle nature of matter. The classic example is that of position and momentum. If we think of a particle riding a wave like a surfer, we could take a snapshot of its position, but this would eradicate any description of its momentum as it would be a still shot and momentum, as we know, is a measurement of movement. Likewise, if we measure the momentum of our surfing particle, we could not say where it is exactly as the particle would be in constant motion, thus eradicating the possibility of discerning its precise position.

This constitutes an inherent conflict of opportunity. We cannot know both the position and momentum of a particle at any given time. We are therefore resigned to regard the two quantities as simultaneously unknowable. Heisenberg demonstrates that the more we know about one value, the less we can know about the other. His mathematical and experimental testing has proved infallible. This is probably the most ontologically challenging idea physicists have ever faced. The very ground upon which we are walking can no longer be reduced to a single objective substrate.

It is this uncertainty that is responsible for the strange results of the double-slit experiment and not, as was previously assumed, the introduction of light. Pairs of properties such as energy and time, as well as position and momentum, are expressions of what we now refer to as wave-particle duality. This theory proposes that a description of matter as a wave or a particle will not suffice by itself and that we must shift from an 'either/or' attitude to a 'both/and' view. As Einstein stated, 'It seems as though we must use sometimes the one theory and sometimes the other, while at times we may use either. We are faced with a new kind of difficulty. We have two contradictory pictures of reality; separately neither of them fully explains the phenomena of light, but together they do.'

A Cat and a Box

Einstein was not very comfortable with this idea. Although it was one of the ideas in the publications that won him the Nobel Prize, he remained one of its greatest opponents. He was supported in his challenging view by Erwin Schrödinger, who proposed a famous thought experiment, which ridiculed the wave-particle duality view.

By the mid-twentieth century, there were two camps in discussions of the qualities of matter: those who were considered to be of a more mystical persuasion and those who adopted the more conventional view of an objective world although Heisenberg would likely have been offended by the term mystical.

Heisenberg's colleague, although a pragmatist in many ways, was also a very intuitive thinker. His name was Niels Bohr and it was he who gave us the term 'complementary' to describe the way in which the conflicting properties of particles were behaving. It was his view that there was no conflict between the properties but rather a kind of harmonic expression that called for a restructuring of our view of reality. The coining of this new term is indicative of just how much emphasis he placed on the use of language when discussing this problem.

Schrödinger and Einstein often found themselves on the other side of the argument, although they agreed that the results of quantum mechanical experimentation were indicative of either an error or inadequate understanding. Quantum physics had an oneiric texture to it and these were men of a positivist persuasion.

Both sides felt passionate about their position and a series of thought experiments were devised by both camps in order to discredit the opposing position. One of the most famous of these is known as Schrödinger's Cat.

The 'cat in a box' experiment was intended only as a side-line discussion of Einstein's famous 1935 EPR article, which was named after its authors, Einstein, Podolsky and Rosen. The trio forged alliance in an attempt to overthrow what had become known as the Copenhagen interpretation of quantum physics. This latter term reflects Bohr and Heisenberg's position that quantum mechanics does not yield an objective description of reality but instead deals only with the probabilities of observing and measuring various aspects of matter. In this interpretation, the entities concerned are not considered to fit either the classic model of waves or particles. Prior to the act of observation, proponents of this interpretation consider matter to be not quite here and not quite there, so they describe it as non-local.

Again, language is important here as we are not describing what matter is, but more what it is not. We are not implying, by using the term 'non-local', that matter is anywhere prior to observation. We are merely stating that all we can say is that it is not anywhere in particular. This is consistent with our mathematical description of matter prior to observation as existing only as a probability and not some kind of object.

It was this non-locality that raised the alarm for Einstein as it implied a violation of his special theory of relativity, which tells us that nothing can travel faster than the speed of light. The problem, as was illustrated by the EPR paradox (and several other papers), was something called quantum entanglement. The idea is simple:

it is possible to generate particles in pairs or groups from a similar source in such a way that their quantum states cannot be described independently, but must instead be viewed as a whole or system. The uncertainty principle holds that any measurement on one particle will affect the properties of the rest of the group.

To illustrate this, we need a complementary property to work with, so let's choose something called spin. Spin is a complex mathematical concept but for now we can think of it as the clockwise or anticlockwise movement of a particle around an axis. A measurement that indicates a clockwise motion around one axis of a particle would correlate with an anticlockwise motion around a partner particle of a pair. This is possible because their total spin will always be zero, an inherent implication of the uncertainty principle. The crucial thing to recognise here is that the particle spin, when measured immediately, affects the spin of the other entangled partner. This is stipulated by the uncertainty equation and so it is cemented in the mathematics.

Einstein and his colleagues pointed out that the pair of particles could be separated at arbitrarily large distances. This would mean that taking measurements at one side of the galaxy could impact matter at the other side in an instant, but according to what Einstein had demonstrated years before in his work on space and time, this is simply not possible because his special theory of relativity holds that nothing can travel faster than the speed of light. If two objects on opposite sides of the cosmos influenced each other instantly, Einstein's rule would be violated. This is where the schism occurred between classical or Newtonian physics and quantum physics. Einstein thought that such 'spooky action at a distance' could be explained by our inadequate knowledge of the event. He considered the Copenhagen interpretation to be incomplete and suggested that either there was some hidden interaction between the particles; even though they were separated, or the information about the outcome of all possible measurements was already present in both particles from the get go.

Schrödinger, one of Einstein's greatest allies, was also deeply concerned by this notion of a quantum system not being in any particular state until it was measured. He amplified the implications of this in a well-known thought experiment meant to ridicule the idea. He proposed putting a cat in a steel chamber loaded with a vial of hydrocyanic acid, which would be opened by a hammer that was attached to a very special kind of trigger called a Geiger counter. In a Geiger counter there is a bit of a radioactive substance so small that it can decay in an hour, or not, as the case may be. It has an equal chance of decaying or not decaying in this timeframe. If it does, then the decayed atom will trigger our terrible device and smash the bottle of poison open, thus killing the cat.

Schrödinger wanted to be provocative. He asserted that if we were to take the experiment seriously, it would imply, by virtue of the entangled state of the cat and the decaying atom, that there must be a kind of superposition for the cat as well as the atom and that both must exist in some kind of indeterminate state before we open the box. So in theory the cat would be both alive and dead at the same time. This is a hard pill to swallow, especially for those who are wedded to the notion of an objective reality.

The world we live in does not seem indeterminate to us. The idea of the world not being there when we are not observing it strikes us as preposterous. It is for these reasons that quantum physics as a scientific party trick by some. It has no bearing on reality *as we know it* and this is the problem.

There can be no doubt that quantum mechanics is a solid theory, as it is consistent, both mathematically and experimentally. To say it gives us a thorough description of nature, however, would seem unjustified as it does not offer any tangential avenue that links up to our own personal experience. It is for this reason that many are quick to disregard the implications of quantum physics. Many scientists are still trying to make sense of this quantum calamity, but the answer they seek may not be what nature has on offer. The idea of an objective world where things run in a precise and mechanical way may soon be resigned to the annals of the past, much the same way the idea of a flat world was done away with once upon a time.

There are two schools of thought amongst the physics community. The first group does not worry about the ontological crisis that science faces. These are the people who make technology by using what we call the quantum cookbook. They are not concerned by what it all means but rather by what we can do with it. Professor David Mermin of New Haven, Connecticut, represents this view in his famous quotation, 'If I were forced to sum up what the Copenhagen interpretation says to me, it would be *Shut up and calculate!*' He has a point. You do not need to venture too far down the rabbit hole to make use of quantum mechanics. You can simply accept it and go from there.

A good example of this is the use of the uncertainty principle to create the technology we use to speak to each other every day – the transistor. This device requires the use of a form of real quantum magic called tunnelling. The theory is simple. Imagine you want an electron to cross an otherwise impenetrable barrier. With your newfound knowledge of wave-particle duality, you might consider setting up the barrier so the distribution curve of your wave function lies partly outside your barrier. Remember you have not put any electron anywhere as you are dealing with a partially hypothetical essay at this point. When you make an observation, however, you cause the wave function to collapse and, in doing so, precipitate an electron particle. If we have set up our apparatus properly, then, although it is on the lower end of the probability scale, we will sometimes have an electron precipitated outside the barrier, as dictated by the collapse of the wave function in this area of the distribution curve. In essence, we are passing electrons across a barrier in a manner that would be impossible in the classic model of physics. This is quantum physics at work in the everyday world, with real consequences.

The alternative view of quantum theory, of which I am a proponent, is that it does matter how we philosophically accommodate our findings. The notion that we cannot experience the strange world of uncertainty and all of its implications is one I would like to challenge with my own personal encounters in the dream world. I have walked through walls, travelled through time and turned my mind inside out, all because I was aware that I was the observer and the object at the same time. Lucid dreaming may be the bridge that science is seeking, the one that will take us to the Promised Land, where fact and fiction can finally merge.

Quantum theory presents us with the opportunity to build a new model of reality, one which does not assume the world was born from a chemical climax that took place billions of years ago. This new model could be far more entangled with our own consciousness, in the same way a dream is. The paradox of the dreamer is that there is no dream without the dreamer, much as there is no dreamer without the dream. The one implies the other. Can we think of matter in a similar fashion? We may soon discover that we cannot separate the subject from the object. The world that was once thought of as being all around us may actually be just as much inside our minds.

This shift will require a complete revision of how we think about the here and now. We will have to traverse some troublesome ideological territory along the way. As a lucid dreamer, I am taking it upon myself to build an original model of consciousness that does not stand in the way of physics but instead complements it. Much as I might try to validate my perspective with personal experience, I am aware of the limitations of this and so I urge the reader to have their own experiences too.

I will offer some insight into my experience of lucid dreaming, but I do not consider this a formal training manual. My chief concern is not to offer a conclusion as to how the world works, but instead to prompt debate, so we may all expand our collective consciousness. This will require an open mind, as well as an appetite for self-discovery, so let's take the next step by asking who exactly is this observer that causes the wave function to collapse.

4) If a Tree Falls

As a magician, my foremost duty has always been to understand the nature of perception, so I can use my understanding to deceive my audience into seeing what I want them to see. But there is an undertone to my devious performance. I play the part of a mouse and the audience plays the role of the surveying cat, waiting to pounce and expose my wicked ways at any moment. The whole experience gives great insight into the nature of how we think and intuit reality.

Contrary to popular belief, however, it is not down to the speed of the magician's hands. An expert magician employs misdirection, which is far more subtle. To misdirect means to guide somebody's attention to the wrong place at the right time. Notice how I used the term 'guide'. This distinguishes it from the act from forcing somebody to look somewhere, as a school kid might, by shouting 'Look over there!' and pointing one way as they run the other. This is what we call distraction and it is far too heavy-handed an approach for a good magician.

The key to good magic is to know that it does not take place in your hands but in the audience's mind. In order for the magic to be effective, it is imperative that what the audience sees feels rational to them. For every action, there is an implied undercurrent of activity. For example, if I were to clench my fist in an attempt to conceal an object then the audience would suspect that I was making an effort to hide something and the game would be up. I therefore keep my hand relaxed in order to get something past them. By the same token, I might sometimes purposely rely on the inference of what an unnaturally posed hand would imply to them when really there is nothing hidden in that hand at all. What I am trying to conceal, or transport from one place to another, can then make its journey in my other hand, which is by now unheeded by my audience. I will later reveal that the cramped hand is empty, at which point the sleight of hand will already have been performed. There is a kind of double deception going on here as I am relying on the audience's assumptions about magic tricks in order to misdirect them from what I am actually doing.

Kids, however, have a certain visual advantage over me when I perform as they don't have a very rigid model of reality, so they do not over-commit their point of view to any single action I perform. They survey everything I do, with no assumptions about what I might be up to. My magic tricks have been busted by more kids than adults, which is why I tend to avoid having them as an audience.

What we can draw from this is that when we over-commit to our view of how the world works, it is easy for us to miss what is really going on. In order to hone our view of reality, we need to ask the right questions, but we can only achieve this if we are willing to abandon some of our existing ideas. We must be open to ideas that challenge our model of nature and we must be sufficiently ontologically flexible to see the signs when they are staring us in the face.

What could serve as a better example of our blindness to the obvious than the prevailing attitude to dreaming? Despite overwhelming evidence suggesting that what we are experiencing is not the ordinary world, we find ourselves hopelessly lost in the inconceivable narrative of the dream. The lucid dreamer has perhaps adopted the child's perspective by noticing how the world is behaving rather than being transfixed by what is happening. A recent German study written about in the *Journal of Sleep Psychology* reported lucid dreaming in 58% of 6-year-olds, compared to 7.1 % in 19-year-olds. I often hear from other lucid dreamers that they had a lot more insight into and control over their dreams in their younger years.

Buddhists, too, talk about the enlightened state of consciousness as being akin to the mind of a child. They say that a great 'un-knowing' emerges in the person, which results in worries being abandoned.

I feel that our 'grown-up' definition of reality prevents us from comprehending the deeper levels of our world and its false assumptions about nature make us feel trapped in our personal experience. There is so much to be gained from opening ourselves up to the dream of life. We just have to be willing to temper the rigorousness of our views.

That Question

One man who has dared to look beyond the known and contemplate the seemingly impossible is the American physicist John Archibald Wheeler. As well as his more practical contributions to general relativity and nuclear fission, he was intrigued by the more theoretical side of science. He coined the term 'wormhole' in reference to a potential shortcut between any two points in space and time. This concept of the wormhole features in so many sci-fi films nowadays.

Perhaps Wheeler could have ventured a credible answer to George Berkeley's famous philosophical question, 'If a tree falls in a forest and no one is there to hear it, does it make a sound?' The answer, according to our current speculation of quantum physics, might be that 'If there is no one there to witness it, then there is no tree.'

Preposterous though this may seem, if we consider this idea through the lens of a dream we can make some sense of it. Dreaming, unlike what we define as the physical world, may not have the same layers as the 'real' world, as we have previously seen.

In dreams, what you see is what there is. If there was no dreamer to see the tree, then there would be no tree to speak of, let alone any sound to hear. One might even alter the original question to 'If a tree falls in a dream and there is no dreamer, is there a dream at all?'

One might argue that the difference between a dream tree and a physical one is the history of the physical tree. In the dream, we do not need a history to qualify the prevailing circumstances and hence do not speak of space and time in an ordinary (or orderly) fashion. I often dream of my house, which was built circa 1850, but I doubt the bricks in my dream house have the same vintage; it is more likely that they have just come into being. They are, as far as I know, only present in the instant I observe them. Once I direct my attention elsewhere, they simply cease to be.

We would not expect to be the case with our tree in the 'real' world as we know trees fall all the time without people there to witness them. We could hypothetically record the section off part of a forest and leave it unobserved for 1,000 years or so, at which time we could revisit and reassess. If a tree had fallen (which would almost certainly have happened), this would, in effect, contradict the above hypotheses of quantum theory.

This presents an alarming dichotomy between what we witness in the everyday world and that which is proposed by both the experimental outcomes of quantum mechanics and my dream world model. The data gathered at the sub-atomic level presents a very different model of reality from what we normally perceive of as our reality, so we end up with cognitive dissonance between the two, at least on the surface. This disharmony, however, is just a gap in our understanding and not some irresolvable argument between the two schools of physics, as it is often framed. Whether we want to admit it or not, activity on the quantum scale is fundamentally entangled with the macro world as what happens to the very small must have consequences for the very big. Thus, we must find a way of accommodating this strange idea that history might in fact be some kind of illusion of the present, as is the case in dreams.

Delaying the Decision to Choose

John Wheeler proposed a number of thought experiments to deal with our dimensional dilemma. These are known collectively as Wheeler's delayed choice experiments. He sought to make sense of the ambiguous nature of light. Light, as we know, shares the same property of wave-particle duality as all matter. At this scale we refer to the little parts of matter as quanta so as not to commit to any particular expression of the matter (remember we cannot actually say whether they are particle- or wave-like in their behaviour until we make a measurement). This is where we get the term quantum physics from. We refer to the quanta of light as photons. It was Wheeler who asked whether or not photons might somehow be able to sense what kind of experimental apparatus we had set up in our double-slit experiment (i.e. whether there was a viewing device, and hence an observer, present or not).

This casts the photons as sensitive to the presence or absence of our viewing technology and capable of behaving or misbehaving accordingly. Remember that when we introduced the detection equipment, the electron adopted particle-like behaviour and when we chose not to view the apparatus; it assumed wave-like behaviour.

Wheeler wanted to know if the photon could sense the design of the experimental apparatus and behave accordingly or if it remained in an indeterminate state until it was observed. In other words, was the decision to act as a wave or particle taken by the photon at the outset of the experiment or was it taken only when the observation was made by our measuring technology? In the latter case, then we have a time paradox to consider as a decision taken in the present moment would be determining past behaviour.

Imagine we had a double-slit experiment set up over a vast distance and did not make any observation of whether or not it behaved as a particle or wave. We would assume from our previous experiments that it would behave as though it were a wave of potentials. Now let's imagine that the time needed for the wave of potentials to travel from the two slits to our detector screen was very long, giving us the opportunity to do something appalling. After the wave of potentials has passed through the slits and begun making its way towards the detector screen, we sneak in and place a detector above the slits. This would normally force the quanta to assume particle-like behaviour. We have changed the experimental design after the photon has made its decision about whether to act as a wave or particle. If the photon behaves in a wave-like manner, then this is consistent with the world as we experience it because the past affects the future in a logical manner and common sense prevails. We might hear the more materially inclined physicists flooding the streets, cheering that causality has been preserved. If, on the other hand, we do not discover an interference pattern but instead two vertical bands of activity, this would mean our view of reality was seriously flawed. The bands would indicate particle-like behaviour, which would imply that the photon had not made its decision to act as a particle or wave until a measurement was made. In other words, the photon would have passed through the double-slit screen in a super-state and would not behave in any precise manner until we observed it.

The implications of this are staggering as it would mean the history of an event in the past could be determined by the manipulation of circumstances in the present. This resonates with our description of dream reality, whereby my house has no history or existence until I observe it in the present, at which time its hypothetical past is implied in some way. I must stress that the past I am referring to in my dream is akin to that of the photon in that it is not a solid past that has taken place but more an inferred past that supports my current experience.

The question is, have we devised such an experiment and, if so, then what was the outcome? Any experiment designed to determine the activity of quanta would be limited by the complementarity principle. Simply stated, this is the notion that *a material body could either behave as a wave or a particle but not both at the same time.* The uncertainty principle infers that any measurement we make collapses the wave function and hence reduces our choice to a particle. It was not until 1982 that an experimental breakthrough was proposed by a sensational duo of scientists, Scully and Druhl, who suggested that it would be possible to mark the path the particle took (through the top or bottom slit) in such a way that one could distinguish which slit was taken at a later stage in the experiment. As we would expect, this would trigger a collapse of the wave function, which of course it does, but what Scully and Druhl proposed was that the which-path (which-slit) information could subsequently be destroyed to cause an interference pattern to reappear. By not knowing which path was taken, we would have made no measurement and hence would not have precipitated the particle behaviour.

A basic experimental set up for this would be to have a single photon hit, what we call a beam splitter. This device is used instead of the double-slit apparatus as it will split the photon or its probability wave and will send an average of 50% of the photons off at a 90-degree angle by reflection and allow the other 50% to pass straight through. So the photons are sent along two paths at 90 degrees to each other, but we want them to reach a common detector. For this we use 45-degree mirrors to turn the two beams towards each other. We end up with a square, one corner of which contains the photon source (laser). The opposite corner contains the detector. In the illustration overleaf (Figure 1), we see the set-up with two different paths indicated – path A exits vertically and path B leaves along horizontal axis.

The detector, or detectors, becomes activated when photons interact by exiting either through the side or vertically through the top. We can distinguish which path was taken by the photon when we examine the result – a click on the vertical detector screen indicates path A and the horizontal detector screen tells us that path B was taken. So we are essentially marking the paths of

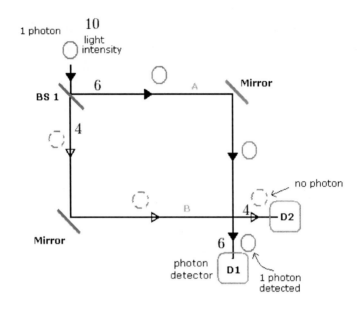

Figure 1

the photons. Now let's take a look at how we can erase this path information and what this erasure yields for us.

In order to achieve this, we introduce a second beam splitter and place it in the same corner as the detector. This acts on both of the entering paths of photons, allowing 50% straight through and 50% to be deflected at 90 degrees (see Figure 2). This destroys the which-path information by sending extra photons from the opposing path to both exits, in effect rendering the marking process useless. We are no longer able to say which path the photon has come from, regardless of the exit it takes. This erasure of the path information precipitates an interference pattern (see Figure 2).

This model design is defined as a quantum eraser experiment. There are many types of these experiments as well as variations on the theme, one of which is of particular interest to us – the delayed choice quantum eraser experiment. But first let's revise our position in order to see how this experiment can be applied and why it is so important to our understanding of quantum physics and also the relationship I propose exists between the quantum and the dreaming state.

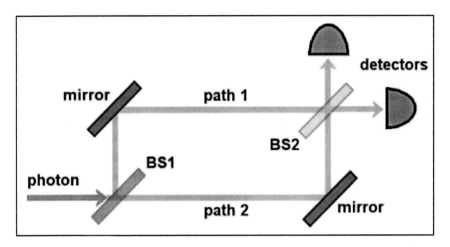

Figure 2

I want to bring your attention back to my earlier question about discovering who the observer is. We must first reiterate a few crucial details – we have discovered that matter, when reduced, can be regarded as tiny bits called quanta. These bits can behave like particles or waves, depending on when we decide to record their activity. The waves are not *real* waves but mathematical inferences representing the potential places where we might find a particle if we took a measurement. It is only when we take the measurement that the matter adopts particle-like behaviour. This is not a reflection of our measuring technology but a result of the inherent uncertainty of matter.

These discoveries have led us to think about matter in new and interesting ways. We no longer think of it as being anywhere in particular, so we use the term 'non-local' to describe its behaviour. This non-locality is more than just a scientific theory. We apply it to design the technology that drives the world today, as in transistors.

Perhaps the most remarkable discovery was quantum entanglement – that is, when two or more particles are generated in such a way that the quantum state of each particle cannot be described independently, so they must be considered as a system or a whole. Again, the uncertainty principle stipulates this and it has been experimentally proven by what is known as the violation of Bell's inequality (see below).

With regards to entanglement, we previously noted that certain complementary properties cannot be spoken of alone, one of which we call spin. We saw how two entangled particles at hypothetically massive distances (many light years apart) would still hold a total spin of zero and hence any random measurement we take of one would instantly tell us the measurement of the other. Einstein's theory of special relativity stands in stark contrast to this as it holds that nothing can travel faster than the speed of light. He suggested that there must be a hidden variable, a connection between the two particles that is simply beyond our observation capabilities. If true, this would mean the theory of special relativity would have been preserved and locality would have prevailed. But in 1964 Irish physicist and philosopher John Bell presented his ground-breaking paper 'On the Einstein-Podolsky-Rosen Paradox'. He had devised a theorem that allowed the argument to be experimentally satisfied finally. Our final group of notary scientists, John Clauser and Stuart Freedman (1972), as well as Alain Aspect et al. (1981), showed that the quantum mechanical model was complete and that entanglement was a demonstrable property of matter, even at seemingly impossible distances.

There has been, and continues to be, a great deal of debate about what this means. We are dealing with a new view of reality whereby there are situations when one cannot discuss any particular part of a system without considering the impact it has on the rest, regardless of the distances involved. Does this mean that some information is travelling faster than the speed of light? To answer the question, we must ask what constitutes speed. The answer is both distance and time. This can be further examined by employing a quantum eraser delayed choice experiment.

This experiment involves shooting a laser at our double-slit screen. As the photon leaves either of the slits, it is passed through a special kind of crystal which causes it to split into two identical, orthogonally polarised entangled photons. This results in a four-horse race consisting of two possible paths depending on which slit they exited from.

We now cause the paths of the four photons to diverge by deflecting them through a Glan-Thompson prism (a special kind of light splitter). One photon from either slit makes their way to a detector screen; we call this pair the signal photons. The other two photons, which are entangled with the signals, make their way towards another prism where they diverge according to which slit they left (A or B). This pair is referred to as the idler photons. They potentially offer us information about which path has been taken. Each of these is sent to detectors via beam splitters, causing them to arrive at a total of four different screens.

However – and this is crucial – we now employ a series of beam splitters and mirrors to erase the path information of two of the detector screens. This is a rather elaborate set-up but the principle is the same as that shown above in Figure 2. We use a beam splitter (or in this case three beam splitters) to saturate two of the screens with photons, potentially arriving from either slit and so creating an interference pattern. As a result, we don't know which slit was employed and hence the which-path information is erased. By contrast, two of the other detector screens are also being hit, but they give us a specific indication of which path was chosen – one screen will indicate slit A and the other slit B.

So far, we have used a classical set-up but now we set up the experiment so the signal and the idler photon arrive at their respective detectors at an arbitrary time difference (for example, eight nanoseconds apart). We also need a coincidence counter. This indicates when a signal and idler photon hit their respective detector screens simultaneously. The eight nanosecond difference would be taken into account, so we can discriminate between entangled photons and the 'background noise', which does not concern us. This allows us to speak about the entangled signal and idler photons in a fluent manner (See Figure 3).

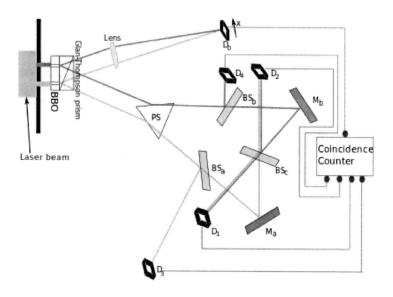

Figure 3

The photon potentially enters either of two slits. It is then split into two entangled pairs (this of course is all hypothetical and does not actually happen until we make a measurement). The photons enter a beam-splitting prism and are sent off in two different directions. One pair, known as the signal photons, makes its way to a detector screen while their entangled partners, the idler pair, make their way to another beam splitter that directs them into a system of beam splitters and mirrors, ending with four different detector screens. These four screens give us two different outcomes to consider. Two of the screens tell us which slit and path were taken, whereas the other two give us an interference pattern to indicate that the 'which-path information' has been erased. Crucially, there is a time delay between the signal and idler photon detection. The whole apparatus could theoretically be set up over a vast distance and the corresponding time delay prolonged for years because the principle effect is the same, regardless of the scale.

Real Magic

There are three parts to every magic trick. The first part is known as the *pledge* and involves the magician showing you something ordinary. Next comes the *turn*, when reality is twisted to show something less ordinary. The final part is the *prestige*, which is when you look for the secret …

The delayed choice we make erasing the path information may not reveal the secret but it does gives us more of a clue about where we should look. When we run the experiment to its conclusion and look at our signal detector, there is a combination of interference and non-interference activity. As they are entangled with photons that have both erased and non-erased information paths, this is the logical outcome. So a photon that is entangled with the erased path would give an interference pattern while the signal photon that is entangled with the known path idler would result in a particle-like impact on our detector. This is verified by use of the coincidence counter, which indicates precisely when we hit both detectors, with the appropriate time delay factored in.

The problem is that the photon arrives at the signal detector and makes a decision to behave as a wave or particle. But its entangled partner, which arrives at the idler detector eight nanoseconds later can decide to erase the path information after the effect and so make the signal change its behaviour to that of a wave. This means that a decision made in the future affects the past. This is verified by our experimental data, whereby a congruent mirroring of wave-

and particle-like behaviour is forged by each of the entangled pair. Regardless of the distance or time, the two partners behave the same way, even if one part of the pair is forced to change its behaviour in the future after its comrade has already made a final decision about its expression.

This is the point at which space and time can come undone for any of us who take this seriously. It prompts speculation of all sorts, though some ideas are more credible than others. Quantum physics is real, but it needs to be interpreted in the appropriate way. It is not, as some people perceive it, a licence to talk crazy. It is, however, worth asking if we are really talking about time travel. When we talk about time, we say that an event now causes something to happen in the future. Something that happens in the future and impacts on the past is termed *retro-causality*. So are we preserving causality with our experiment or not? There are countless debates, theories and arguments for or against this point of view, but no definite answers. However, we should pay attention to something crucial here: we can only observe the interference pattern on the signal detector after we examine the idler screens.

We can only ever witness the interference patterns retrospectively when we make a decision to erase the data. In truth, we do not normally see interference isolated on the signal detector screen; it only ever forms part of a pattern of photons. This is due to a phase shift in the waves after they have been passed through our optical crystal (the one that split them into entangled pairs). This causes them to mark the screen in such a manner that we do not ordinarily see interference patterns but instead infer it from our coincidence counter and the interference pattern of the entangled idler partners. So, until a measurement of the idler is taken, we cannot say that there is any proof of the event that allegedly occurred eight nanoseconds previously.

This brings us back to our opening discussion about how we perceive events in dreams. What we witness in the dreaming present implies a pseudo-past, but we do not think a real event has taken place. As an example, I might see a tree in my dream, which might imply that a seed was once planted in the ground, after which roots spread and branches grew, but this was not necessarily the case as it is a dream tree. *This experience of the tree in the dream present implies a hypothetical past, which is a function of the present and not an event unto itself.*

Dreams do not have to be built on solid historical foundations and yet there is an inferred hypothetical past to the dreamscape. What we discover at the heart of nature, whether we are willing to accept it or not, is the notion that causality and locality are only ever a product of our current observation, that it is the act of measuring that precipitates reality as we know it. Even when we employ machine technology to act as the measuring device, it is only when either you or I engage it with our senses that particle-like behaviour is triggered. The idea that the machine can collapse the wave function is a common misinterpretation. Until the conscious being interacts with the system, there is no information to speak of.

This is well illustrated by the delayed choice quantum eraser experiment as we know that there is an inferred machine recording being made prior to our interaction with the machine, but this is subject to change according to our apparently latter measurement. It is this kind of retrograde event determination that places us, the conscious observer, at the centre of our world as whatever we are witnessing is only ever revealed to be here and now, as in a dream. Whether one agrees or not, it seems inevitable that the physics of the future will concern the very thing that is querying the subject: consciousness. The age-old mind-body problem has found a new home in the world of the quanta. It is a place where thought and matter have forged an alliance, where time and space no longer have a precise meaning, as vast distances are travelled with a total disregard for the clock.

Although there is much more to discover and debate, for me at least, reality is plastic. It can bend and fold. When you know you are dreaming, it can even be broken on occasions to reveal an infinite vastness. I often wonder whether the likes of Schrödinger ever considered what a quantum world would look like – a place where alive-dead cats are given a home to roost; a place where here is there and there is here; a place where space and time are mere concepts to be played with.

As we abandon the body to enter the deepest recesses of the mind, I cannot help but feel that the general resignation of dreams to the field of psychoanalysis, and even psychological trickery, may have been premature. As a lucid dreamer, I can see how we are at a crossroads in our understanding and experience of consciousness, but the path is clear. We conscious dreamers are the Marco Polos of the mind. Our task is to saddle up and wonder at our world as we march off into the wide open arms of infinity …

5) The Dream Lab

Einstein once said that you cannot solve a problem with the same consciousness that created it. Having considered the chief dilemma faced by physicists today (i.e. that the micro and macro world behave in very different ways), it is interesting to note that despite the friction between these two models, we still employ the same umbrella term 'matter' when talking about either. Although we cannot locate the transition point between the micro and the macro world exactly, we take it to be somewhere around the molecular to atomic boundary, though we do not draw a distinct line. Moreover, we do not talk about the two worlds as mutually exclusive entities; instead, we seek a theory that will ultimately unify them.

This is the holy grail of physics: a single theory of everything that can describe matter as a whole. Progress is being made in this direction as quantum phenomena are being exhibited by progressively larger bodies of material. Perhaps there will come a day when we can walk through walls and traverse space and time through wormholes. Some scientists disagree and state that the qualities of the sub-atomic world can have no bearing on our level of reality, but perhaps they are of the same ilk as the scientists who speculated that being aware of the fact that one is dreaming was a psycho-physiological impossibility.

In a world in which precedence is increasingly being given to personal experience, we must revise our view of what might actually be achievable. As a lucid dreamer, I believe that what I have to contribute to current thinking about reality is extremely valuable, even if it is inherently subjective. I feel that the frame we have created for consciousness in our current model is lacking. The prevailing view holds that consciousness is something that happens in our heads and that it is the exclusive job of the brain to compose and construct the world we live in. This is as narrow-minded an idea as the suggestion that Guns N' Roses must be in your radio because when you break the radio you can no longer hear them.

People often say, 'It's not real; it was just a dream', or, 'It's just your imagination'. I agree that it may have been a dream or one's imagination but what exactly is the imagination? That is the question. Our current view insists on a differentiation between 'reality' and 'the imagination'. As someone who has spent a great deal of time investigating the world from the perspective of lucid dreams, I cannot support such a distinction. I believe that consciousness can express itself in two apparently different ways, in the same way that matter does (quantum and classic mechanics). And as with matter, regardless of the outward expression of the event what remains constant is the presence of you and me, the observing witness.

Dreams are certainly different to waking life, at least on the surface, but that is not to say they are made of different materials. If we are to seriously consider the idea that matter can exist in different phases and that these phases, although different in their measurable expression, still imply an underlying mutual matrix, then surely we must extend the same courtesy to consciousness. If such a relationship could be demonstrated, I would expect the lucid dream state to act as a kind of conduit between the dreaming and waking states, allowing us to investigate such a hypothesis.

The Four Cardinal Distinctions

I began my inquiry by contrasting dreaming and waking. What are the fundamental experiential differences between the two? There are, by my account, four major distinctions. The first of these is *causality*. The waking world, like the classic world of physics, is built in such a way that the past determines the present. We can confidently say that such a property is not strictly evident in dreaming or at the quantum scale of physics. There is evidence of retro-causality or even non-causality at the quantum scale as we saw in our delayed choice quantum eraser experiment and we married this to our thought experiment of our dream bedroom to show a similar motif here.

My second distinction is *gravity*. In the classical waking world, we do not ordinarily have the ability to fly, but dreaming offers this possibility. This is because the rules of gravity, as we know them, do not strictly apply to dreams. Although we usually walk on the ground rather than the ceiling in our dreams, it is nonetheless possible to walk on the wall, as I did in my first lucid dream. This is only possible because of the opportunity dreaming gives us to manipulate the gravitational glue of the inner world. In the quantum state, we currently lack a precise definition of mass due to the implications of the uncertainty principle. Furthermore, at the quantum scale, although there are a number of new theories making headlines, we still do not have reliable evidence of gravity.

My third essential distinction between waking and dreaming is *a lack of rational insight into our state of consciousness*. When we are dreaming we accept things as they are even if they are all a bit topsy-turvy. Cognitive functioning can also be inferred at the quantum scale because when we have no intuitive observer we cannot take a measurement. The observer in this case too will have to take a more malleable view of their reality, allowing matter to be everywhere, nowhere and probably somewhere all at the same time. This oxymoronic perspective is counter-intuitive to the ordered mind of the classical mechanical dimension of space-time as prescribed by Einstein's equations. This third distinction will be examined in more detail as we progress but for now I would like to emphasise the apparent disregard of the mind for absolute congruency in these two states.

Finally, in dreaming we have *a lack of consensual perspective*. That is to say that what we experience does not ordinarily extend beyond the boundaries of the individual. This, too, will require further discussion as I propose to show how an isolated group of observers may be able to experience a kind of collective dream by entering into a very peculiar state of consciousness under the guidance of a dream director of sorts.

When I first compiled my list, it was immediately apparent how much it mirrored the problems posed by quantum physics. In dreaming there is a lack of causality, no strict gravitational constant, uncertain mass and an observer that somehow ties the whole event together. This last point is key, as when the observer's attention is adequately invested, the world behaves in an orderly way but when it is not, the world becomes a more ambiguous place. As a lucid dreamer, I felt compelled to take this essay into deeper intellectual waters.

Uncertainty and Dreaming

I began where all lucid dreamers should, with a reality check. Probably the most common test we use to distinguish the dream world form the waking world is the finger-through-the-hand test, which is akin to the hand-through-the-wall test. By passing apparently solid matter through a physical barrier, one realises one is dreaming and hence confirms lucidity. One cannot help but remark on the tunnelling of atoms through apparently impossible mediums, as in quantum mechanics, and the fact that there is a certain probability factor at play. In the case of a finger going through one's hand, it is not always easy to perform such a task, especially when one is genuinely unsure of one's situation. Can we infer an uncertainty factor here too?

I recall an incident when I became suspicious that I might be dreaming. I was living in London at the time but suddenly became aware that I was in my old house in Ireland, in a kitchen that had long since been demolished and replaced by a more contemporary one. My friend Sarah, who as far as I know, has never been to Ireland, let alone inside my old house, was washing dishes in the kitchen. There was enough evidence for me to realise that something didn't add up, so I took a moment to reflect before skipping over to my friend and saying, 'Hey Sarah, we're dreaming, you're in my dream!'

I felt pretty sure that this was true, but she replied, 'No we're not!' This did not deter me. By now I was brimming with confidence that I was dreaming, so I protested, 'Look, I will prove it to you!' I ran and jumped at the wall, intending to leap right through it. However I bounced back like a ping-pong ball. I picked myself up, but I had lost any sense of lucidity. It was not until the next morning that I realised I had missed an opportunity to dream lucidly. Why had I failed to jump through the wall?

For me, when I think I am dreaming, I usually am. Often I don't even have to perform a reality check, but I do so anyway, just in case I do something silly like jump off a building. But even when I am certain I am dreaming, the reality check can fail. Most lucid dreamers brush this off but I believe it is an important irregularity that has something to do with the influence of mind over matter.

As an example, it had become apparent to me that walls in dreams sometimes allowed me to walk through them and sometimes they did not. On average, jumping through walls was more successful than walking through them, but this sometimes resulted in me bouncing off the wall as there seems to be a kind of elasticity to the dream matrix that prevents injury. I never suffered pain and didn't break any bones but I did uncover a pattern that would take me deeper down the rabbit hole of self-discovery.

I would either jump head first (as if I were jumping off a diving board) or charge at the wall with my shoulder. The head-first jump had a higher success rate that the shoulder method, so it would seem that my psychological set-up was impacting the physics of the dream. A head-first jump suggested a kind of confidence whereas the shoulder, in hindsight, indicated a kind of subtle apprehension, which I believe, impacted the texture of my world. Psychological expectation affected the physical dynamics of the dream. I wanted to model this in a repeatable way. I needed to devise an experiment that anyone could repeat while dreaming, an experiment that would lead to numerical data to crunch in the hope of achieving a better understanding of the nature of dreaming reality.

The Experiment

I go to the gym regularly and I can easily do about fifty push-ups, at which point I start to grow fatigued. One day I asked myself, 'How many push-ups I could do in a dream?' It was a profound question as it dealt with whether or not I would feel the weight of my body in a dream, as well as what gravitational intercourse this might have with the dreamscape. I also felt that it met the criteria for my dream experiment as it was repeatable and possible to perform in any dream by anyone who had the lucid insight to attempt it. Moreover, it would produce some kind of numerical outcome.

My first attempt at the experiment was an interesting affair as I did not know what to expect. I was concerned about what I had come to define as 'expectation contamination', the notion that whatever I expected to happen in a dream would affect the outcome, even if I didn't want it to. As my body posture seemed to limit or aid my ability to jump through walls, I was careful not to allow myself to be affected by a similar psychological bias with my push-up posture. I chose to adopt a neutral position; I would get onto my hands and just start pushing up and down, as I ordinarily do in the gym.

This was a radical experiment. I was testing a hypothesis about dreaming by making measurements inside the dream.

It did not take long for me to avail of the opportunity to begin my inquiry. I became lucid in my bedroom as I had many times previously. I reality-checked successfully on my first finger through hand attempt and proceeded to find a suitable area to perform my exercise. I entered the lounge of my house, which seemed familiar and solid. I readied myself, cleared my mind of any expectation and began to do push-ups…

On the first push upwards I floated off the ground. It was as if I was on the moon. I drifted back down towards the floor and landed unevenly. When I tried a second time, I floated off the ground – feet and hands. I drifted about one foot off the ground before falling back onto my hands again. A third attempt was made. It was now clear that this was a low-gravity environment, not unfamiliar territory for a lucid dreamer. For the most part, gravity behaves normally in dreams but when we become aware of the fact that we are dreaming, we experience a lack of 'pull' between our body and the environment. This is why one of the first activities many lucid dreamers perform upon lucid insight is flight.

This weightlessness is a familiar feeling for me. It is what I was alluding to earlier when I said that I normally realise I am dreaming before I even perform a reality check. It is usually this familiar sense of floating that catches my attention and triggers lucidity. This low-gravity effect halted my push-up experiment in its tracks. After ten push-ups, I determined that my experiment had failed due to the prevailing conditions.

My second, third and fourth attempts at push-ups in the lucid dream state were more banal experiences in that the dream was a lot more like the waking world. I was able to perform the push-ups with a kind of gravitational feedback. I was even slowed down on all three occasions after about thirty push-ups. Fatigued and weighed down by the weight of my body, I could not do more than about forty push-ups. I was perplexed as this outcome was almost the reverse of the outcome of initial experiment. But I had what any good scientist wants: a comparison study yielding two different results. If I could find a third, I would have enough data to pick out a common thread and see how manipulating it might affect the experiment.

I speculated that such a finding would help me get a better picture of this elusive state of consciousness. My experiment contained four key elements: mass; gravity; probability; and me, the conscious observer. As with a quantum experiment, nothing could be isolated and analysed alone. Everything had to be considered as an entangled system. But I was certain the experiment would bring me closer to defining the relationship between physics and consciousness.

Dreaming is too often consigned to the bookshelves of half statements and conjecture. It is not regarded as hard science, which is to say that it is not possible to repeat precise dream experiments, so scientists find it difficult to offer any data on the subject. Some people disregard dreaming as any kind of true reality on this basis. I often hear statements like, 'Dreams are not real', but how can we take such a statement seriously without any clear definition of what reality is? In my examination of lucid dreaming, I am attempting to offer an insight into how and why things behave the way they do in what we call the unconscious mind.

I knew that answers to some of my questions could be found with the help of the push-ups experiment. I just needed a third kind of outcome. On reflection, my initial feeling about this experiment was that one should be able to perform push-ups indefinitely. When I could not, I was surprised because we are led to believe that dreams are modelled on our expectations. It was as if the dream had some a system akin to the uncertainty factor that troubles the world of physics. I found myself deeply concerned that the dream could behave in such a way. Could there be an uncertainty principle involved in dreams?

The clue to this conundrum was evident in the inconsistency of reality checks, even to the already fully aware lucid dreamer. The dynamics of flying in dreams had also raised a flag for me. I had begun to experiment with flight in some of my previous examinations of dreams. I had varying levels of success but could yet ascribe any specific physical laws to the dream world. It seemed like a nebulous task, one which most people choose to ignore. Dreams, they assume, are thoughts, memories or expectations fired up by an over-active brain, but these notions are empty and unhelpful when one is trying to describe the physical properties of a world which I was able to consciously test and explore. I was certain that the dream world was more real than it was being given credit for. Our inadequate (and most likely misguided) definition of reality was the problem. To justify my definition of the dream world as a form of reality, I needed something testable. I knew my push-ups experiment could help shed some light on the matter.

Although my experiment had been stunted by this new leaden feeling in the body, it was occasionally interrupted by times when I would float. It was only a matter of time before I found that middle place – the infinite push-up workout.

It was during another lucid dream that it happened. I was in my bedroom. I had not reality-checked. I simply decided on becoming lucid that I would perform my experiment. Something felt right. So I began – down, up, down, up, down, up ... On and on it went. After over a hundred push-ups, there was no sign of any fatigue. I sailed past the 200 mark. After 250 push-ups, I stopped, stood up and took a moment to reflect. I could have gone on endlessly and yet I could feel the weight of my body and how it related to the solid ground on which I stood.

The implications were vast and immediate. I was experiencing a harmonious co-creation of mental and physical reality. This delicate construct of matter and mind was conditioned by a kind of volume control switch, which could be turned up and down to apply or release the mass and gravity. The quest was to discover what it was that toggled this sliding scale from low to high and, moreover, what this middle place meant. I was certain I had discovered a version of reality where the laws of matter could be perfectly balanced with the mind, so they could both accommodate the shape and structure of the world and allow it to be infinitely interacted with.

The Atom or the Ape

That the mind can affect the body is hardly ground-breaking news. That the dream world can have flexible physical properties is not headlines either. However, that this mind-body complex could be transformed into a fully functioning model in the dream world that might offer us insight into the nature of consciousness was something interesting indeed. I felt that this model could help us discover more about the relationship between consciousness and physics. After all, what is an atom if there is no one there to perceive it?

How the body and mind are connected presents us with a paradox. We cannot observe the body without the mind, nor can we suggest that there is a mind without a body. So the question is perhaps not, 'Which came first, the chicken or the egg?' but rather 'Which came first, the atom or the ape?' It is us, the apes, who discovered the atom because we are the proprietors of a peculiar type of brain that engineered the technology to find it, but the question remains, are atoms inherent to the universe or are they a product of the evolution of our own consciousness?

The problem we face in physics today is that the data from experiments seems to stand in stark contrast to our experience of everyday life, so we are forced to brush it aside as a symptom of our scientific immaturity. It is widely thought that the inference of retro-causality and non-locality are philosophical fantasies that will soon be ironed out by new theories and, likewise, that consciousness should not affect matter as it is objective in nature.

But it is in the laboratory of the mind that we can encounter all of this quantum weirdness in a first-hand way. The quirkiness of matter and gravity in dreams is something we are all familiar with, but the idea of retro-causality raises eyebrows. To experience it, however, would be life-changing. This was how I felt when I decided to time travel…

Causality is not something we inherently abide by in dreams. We know from our ordinary experiences of dreaming that we can encounter people and places from the past in the present. Some people re-experience earlier periods in their lives and can even become younger versions of their own selves. To do so with lucid insight, however, would offer something unique, so I designed an experiment to facilitate this, one that would not be contaminated by expectation.

The technique I used was inspired by Robert Waggoner, whose book describes how he turns his attention to the dream itself and shouts out requests to what he calls 'the awareness behind the dream'. In my experiment, I perched on the roof of a building and shouted my intention out loud. 'Dream, show me time travel!' As I did so, I launched myself backwards off the ledge and dropped.

Free-falling from the building was my own idea. I wanted to shock the dream into action by giving it a narrative dead end and forcing it to make a decision about what would happen next. I experienced all the visceral sensations of a real fall, but I was certain that I was dreaming (I had reality-checked adequately). The building was tall and surrounded by a deeply trenched basement, so a fall from the top would certainly end in death in waking life.

The dream changed as I plunged. One second I was falling and a split second later I was standing in Ireland, outside of my old house. My parents were seeing off my sister and her boyfriend, who were leaving in their car. I thought the boyfriend was someone I had known once, but I was sure he never dated by my sister. She was younger and so were my parents. I was certain I had travelled back to an earlier time.

I asked my father what year it was. He informed me that it was 1997. I looked him in the eye and said, 'There's something I have to tell you. I'm not who you think I am. This is going to sound impossible but it's true. I am actually Rory from the future. I am currently in London and it's 4 a.m. on 31 August 2009. The technology I am using to be here is known as lucid dreaming, but it's something you will not know about for a few years yet, so you will not remember this after I am gone as lucid dreaming won't be possible for you in your reality.' His expression was one of acceptance, the kind my father adopts when he is pretending to understand something that he clearly doesn't. I bid him farewell and went on my way.

The reason why he would not be able to remember his encounter is known as the *grandfather paradox*. If I travelled back in time and killed my grandfather, I would cease to exist, but then I would never be alive to kill him in the first place. Fortunately for my father and me, my intentions were not so macabre. However I did feel that there was something similarly paradoxical about the interaction; that somehow this retro-active interruption of causality could have an impact on a potential future and yet remain contained by the original past. I imagined a kind of split in the timeline occurring at some later date, when all the possibilities of the equation would be in play together.

My second time-travel encounter was triggered in much the same fashion. I found another tall building, flew to the top and let myself fall off it. Again the dream took the initiative and I found myself standing outside an unfamiliar building. I was greeted by a young man who seemed to recognise me. He looked me in the eye in a kind, professional way and said, 'I think you should meet the 'others.' We entered the large building and made our way into a beautifully polished apartment. I could not date it, but the shiny surfaces made it seem ultra-modern. I would not say that it was futuristic, but the materials shone in a way that seemed strange and unfamiliar.

As I walked towards my hosts, I noticed that there were four glass cases to my right, each one containing what seemed like time-travelling trophies. There was an old torn flag. It was dirty, as if it had been exposed to cannon smoke. Perhaps it was once used to lead a troop into battle. There was a musket in one of the other cases. The third case contained some kind of prehistoric creature. It was about the size of a dinner plate and had an aquatic look. It had the monster-like appearance of certain deep sea creatures and ancient marine life, with teeth that seemed out of proportion to its relatively small body. The fourth case contained a map. It looked antiquated and depicted more sea than land. Perhaps, I thought to myself, the lands that occupied some areas of the world had not yet been discovered or perhaps the land had not even emerged from the oceans yet.

Finally I was in the presence of the others. They seemed guarded, as if I had interrupted them. When I introduced myself, they all glanced at each other and spoke in a kind of psychic language. No mouths moved and there was silence, but it was clear that they were all engrossed in mutual discussion. I broke the silence by asking if I could know their names. Again they looked at each other, and then one of them spoke. It was as if he was delivering the group's shared view. He simply said, 'No'. It was clear that they did not to want to negotiate. I felt that I did not meet the requirements for this particular meeting, so I made my excuses and left.

Non-verbal communication in dreams was not new to me. Many lucid dreamers report the use of psychic power in the dream world. I have spoken to people in this psychic manner and these 'conversations' have felt natural and coherent. One might extrapolate that this natural in the dream world as everything in the dream is coming from one source – you. Everything is entangled in everything else. Nothing is truly separate. However, when one actually experiences other people in dreams, they mostly seem to have conscious agency of their own. These others certainly did.

As I reflect on this experience, as well as other incidents of this psychic phenomenon, I think about how it would be impossible to explain the internet to people a few decades ago. I frequently amuse myself walking the streets of London with my hands-free on, speaking to my sisters in Canada, many thousands of miles away. I might even turn the camera on. That such a thing is possible must point the way towards ever increased complexity in our communications. Perhaps it is not so unlikely that we will one day cease to need our mouths for speaking.

Who knows what might be possible in the future? We may achieve the power of unaided flight; space and time might collapse at the press of a button; the idea of causality could become a relic. The question, perhaps, is not what might be possible in the future, but what possibilities exist now that we cannot see clearly because they are outside our understanding of reality? If we are willing to look at dreaming as a physical dimension, then lucid dreaming offers us the opportunity to pull that hypothetical future towards our present.

6) The Mad Scientist

The new world view emerging will, no doubt, be met with resistance, especially while these ideas are still in an embryonic state and the counter views hold such sway with the masses. Those who seek to devalue the relationship between the observer and the reality he or she experiences are insisting on a world believed to be 'out there', which tends to a paradoxical view of reality. Take, for example, something as simple but profound as the beginning of the universe. If we say that it had some kind of a genesis, we must ask from where it came from. In other words, what gave birth to the cosmos?

If we could provide an answer to this question, we would then have to ask, does our answer, too, have a predecessor? This line of questioning results in what we call infinite regress. But I want to propose that this is a by-product of our limited idea of how the world works rather than something that will continue to elude us indefinitely.

The barriers to understanding are not, as Einstein posited, a consequence of ignorance, but in fact due to what we already believe to be true. Relinquishing ideological territory is not something that comes easy to any of us. We are all born and raised in various cultural conditions, which narrows our bandwidth of understanding to fashion our ontological stance. Richard Dawkins makes a great argument for this in his controversial book *The God Delusion*. He describes the motivation for religious belief as being of a geographical heritage rather than being rooted in some deep truth. However, as he points out, this does not dissuade believers. To them it is simply their reality, even, and perhaps especially, when the Dawkins' dilemma is pointed out to them.

The philosopher Terrence McKenna iterated how our social heritage was all that we were ever exposed to. He referred to this as our *cultural operating system*. He compared it to piece of software which is downloaded into the biological hard drive of the Homo sapiens and encourages certain behaviour motifs. He and I believe that none of these operating systems are more or less valuable, in terms of their data. Each system has merit in its own context but is limited in other ways. When these individual systems are forced to interact, they inform and catalyse each other. The internet, McKenna anticipated, would pave the way for a new world and a global consciousness. Other visionaries like the Harvard psychologist and LSD populariser Timothy Leary, anticipated the same eventual outcome. That is, that we will eventually no longer rely on the limitations of disconnected dogmas and instead come to a more eclectic understanding of being.

In my lifetime, I have witnessed the dissolution of religion and politics on many levels. Financial institutions, too, are being encroached upon by online currencies like bit coin and transaction systems like PayPal. In an increasingly virtual world, it may only be a matter of time before larger governing bodies dissolve into the matrix of more elaborate existential enterprises. The value I place on personal experience is not intended to contradict the physical data, but instead to complement it. Surely there is merit in experiencing events that mirror our quantum experiments. It is because we normally do not have access to time travel and non-locality that we so readily dismiss them in the world of the quanta. The cognitive dissonance that such findings imply pushes us back into our rational minds to seek refuge.

We are being held back by our own limited beliefs. Take, as an example, dreaming. Our Western cultural understanding of the world does not allow dreams to step into the guarded halls of physics. But in dreams it is possible to experience psychic entanglement and time travel in a way that insists on a conscious witness in order for events to occur. Dreaming reality is a way of looking at the world.

It is no more or less of a fact than physical reality as they are both cultural constructs of consciousness, as I propose to show you.

Anthropologist Charles D. Laughlin explains in his insightful *Communing with the Gods* that there are two different cultural approaches to consciousness: mono and poly-phasic modalities. In the Western world, we subscribe to the idea that there is one primary state of consciousness and that any other is only ever an altered state of mind, which does not constitute a pure reality in its own right. This is the mono-phasic model of reality and it forms the basis of science. I am attempting to call this model into question in this book. The poly-phasic view, which I, as well as most aboriginal peoples, subscribe to, proposes that what we are experience in dreaming, drug-induced states and the like is not an altered state of consciousness, as in the classic view, but an altered state of reality. This theory holds that all states of consciousness are part of the same spectrum of reality. What varies is the world itself.

Although this may seem like a fantasy, we should ask ourselves how we came to think in this way. Most of what we consider reality is nothing more than a cultural notion, which has been passed down from one generation to the next. Might not other cultural perspectives, radical though they may seem, offer us an insight into the nature of reality? If there is, as I propose, a common thread running through the physical and the dream world, then what might it be?

It is this question that I sought to answer when I first took up lucid dreaming as a means of enquiring into the nature of reality. I concluded, after much experience of lucid dreaming, that the dream world has the same fundamental properties as the material world and that what we witness when dreaming is a kind of quantum state of consciousness, a place where the problems of physics become the playground of possibility and the question of what it means to be human can be explored in a whole new way. This missing factor tying it all together could surely be identified, I was sure of it, but until then I would refer to it as 'Factor X'

Time to Travel Back

There comes a point of no return in any explorer's adventure. I have passed this point. It happened one winter night in 2010, when I took to the dream world once more in order to time travel. I looked for a tall building. I took the stairs this time instead of flying up. This gave me time to ready myself for what I anticipated would be a special experience. I navigated my way out onto a window ledge. I felt my body tip backwards over my heels and I plummeted.

Things were different this time. I was falling into an endlessly swirling tunnel. It was poorly lit but order began to emerge from the pools of smoke that were tumbling towards each other. I noticed how cold the scene looked and remarked that it felt rather neutral in temperature. I was dragged deeper and deeper, feet first, at frantic speed. I did not feel fear. I felt that what I was engaged in would surely amount to some great revelation, if I could just hold onto my sanity for long enough. The last thing I saw was a face forming in the smoke. It looked like a piece of stone art, representing a person from some ancient time. It was vaguely decorative with geometric patterns which encompassed a sense of vastness behind its primitive, widened eyes. It seemed like I was in the presence of an archaic spirit. It was not something I could see, but a feeling I had. I was prepared to let the experience take me. I drifted towards the numinous face and was engulfed by one of its huge hollow eyes.

I was back in my old bedroom in Ireland. It was my childhood room before we converted the house into a two-storey. Staring at me were the faces of two ten-year-old boys: my twin and my younger self. I said to them, 'Don't be afraid. I am Rory from the future and I am here to tell you something very important. You [and I am referring to my younger self now] will one day discover a great secret about your world. Your duty will be to share it and set others free from the prison of their minds.'

The pair looked at me, unperturbed. To be fair, I was one of those children who took the idea of magic seriously. In hindsight, I would say that up until the moment my parents revealed the truth about Santa I firmly believed in the possibility of the impossible. It was during that conversation with my parents that my wings were cut as no Santa meant no magic.

I said goodbye to the twins and decided to wake up, back in my bedroom. I sat upright in my bed and reflected on the encounter. I did not know how to frame it. Had I met my actual self? If so, why couldn't I remember it? And yet I could remember it, but only from my adult perspective. Did this constitute a retro-causal affair? I could not answer any of these questions at the time but I was certain that I had discovered something terrific about my world and I knew that one day soon I would be writing this book with this encounter at the centre of it. Even today, I cannot offer an explanation of the event. Perhaps it will remain a mystery.

As unique as the experience was, I felt that the look on the boys' faces was interesting. It reminded me of my father's expression on my previous time-travel adventure. It was that sense of acceptance of the situation. I could have told my father I was pregnant and he would have accepted it. The boys had that same imperturbable expression, as if even speaking to a four-headed dragon would have made sense to them. I have noticed this expression on the faces of many other dream beings encountered on my travels.

I recall a particular incident when I suggested to a group of people that we were dreaming. They dismissed the comment, but I persisted. 'This is a dream. I will prove it!' I floated up into the air, exclaiming that my ability to fly was proof that I was dreaming. They looked at me as if this was normal and returned to their group chat. I made my excuses and left, although this time I was not discouraged. I knew I was dreaming and went on to have a lucid adventure.

This ability to accept the way the world is, regardless of how insane it might seem is made possible, in part, by the brain's ability to confabulate. When faced with something unusual, the mind can either flag it or fashion a comfortable narrative around it to support the situation. This becomes our reality. But the mind has limitations to how much confabulation it will allow. However, the dreaming mind does not have such limitations. Neither, for that matter, does the hypnotised mind, the child's mind, the drugged mind or the mentally deficient mind. This inability to articulate the architecture of our world would prove to be exactly what I had been looking for. Factor X had reared its head, even if I couldn't see it yet. The question remained: what was this variable that could bridge the gap between the classic material frame of nature and that of the mysterious magical realm? And could it tie quantum physics to altered states of consciousness?

Harvard's professor of psychiatry, J. Allan Hobson, is most famous for his biological model of dreaming. He has written extensively on the subject and has steered us away from the classic psychoanalytic roots of Freud into a more holistic appraisal of the process. As he is qualified in neurophysiology and psychiatry alike, his model of dreaming is not an either-or picture of the brain and mind, but a harmonious view that he refers to as the *brain-mind system*. This is a very important shift in the language frame, as we are moving away from the classic Cartesian dualism of body/mind that has stunted our thinking for so long. The cosmos might be more accurately thought of as an interconnected whole, even if it seems outwardly separate. Although Hobson does not make that leap, he has still moved the prevailing view away from the limited either pure biology or pure psychology. Personally I like to think that this will ultimately extend to physics too, at which point we will begin to bridge the gap between mind and matter.

As a lucid dreamer, I am satisfied that we can experience the matter-mind version of reality, but how we create a language for this will ultimately prove to be the most important task we have to tackle and who could be better qualified than the dreamers who know the lucid world? However, we should not run away with ourselves by throwing out half-baked ideas as theories and expecting people to take them seriously. This is why my appraisal of biology will be built on the same kind of foundation I used to discuss physics, i.e. one based on current scientific thinking.

An Insane Idea

Hobson opens his fascinating book *The Chemistry of Conscious States* with a ground-breaking description of the dreaming mind as being diagnostically akin to *mental deficiency syndrome.* He goes on to analyse a dream recorded by a subject of his known as Delia. She describes her dream adventure and Hobson goes on to perform what is called a *mental status examination.* The MSE, as it is commonly abbreviated, is a very important tool in the practice of psychiatry. It gives us an insight into the patient's current state of consciousness. When combined with the biographical and historical psychiatric history of the person, a better picture of their mental health can be formulated.

Although the assessment of Delia revealed her to be mentally compromised, it was determined that what she was experiencing was an acute form of insanity and not something that needed chronic medical attention. Hobson recognises that the person he was observing was in a state of REM brain activity and that their physical body was paralysed and unable to cause harm (either to the subject or others). But he is nonetheless certain that her behaviour demonstrates a clear picture of mental instability, so he concludes that dreaming is a necessary kind of temporary insanity we all experience every night.

I propose to proceed as Hobson did in order to elaborate upon this diagnosis and shed some light on why the brain has to temporarily give way to nocturnal madness. The following is a dream I recorded in 2013. I was not lucid at the time, nor was I attempting to be. It was a random dream recorded after the event, for the purpose of this appraisal.

I'm travelling on a train with my friend, who happens to be movie star Johnny Lee Miller; he stunt jumps off the train and waves me on as he does so

I reach into my jacket and pull out a silenced revolver and shoot him 3 times in the chest

He has a bulletproof vest on and I see puffs of cotton popping upon impact of each bullet

He looks back at me with a sense of adventure like some kind of James Bond that will pursue me for betraying him …

I am curious about the weapon and nonchalantly explore it by cocking it a couple of times and then shooting out the window as we pass through a tunnel

I find the sound of the silencer quite soothing and muse to myself briefly about that sensation

My phone receives a text from my twin telling me that our friend is in trouble at work for drug use

I look at a newspaper beside me on the train and see that a BBC exec is in trouble for intravenous heroin use at work. I do the maths, realising it's my friend

A ticket inspector arrives and asks for my ticket

I know my ticket probably doesn't get me this far on the line and feel a little apprehensive about showing her so I tell her this is my stop

We are hurtling downhill between two large blocks of cartoon-like buildings with rail tracks scattered in every possible direction

I remark to myself how amazing it is that the train doesn't catch a rogue tack and flip over and take a mild pleasure in the sensation of eminent danger as we speed down the hill towards the next station. I am aware that I have been here before and come back here time and time again as I enjoy the view so much I leave the train and enter a cafe where I place a book on the counter called A Whale of a Time. *Alongside it, I place some of my own written notes and remark to the waiter that it is about a group of environmentalists that steal a whale and that I am researching it for a book I am writing myself*

*I have a frozen pizza ready to place in the oven, one I brought along
with me. I look into the oven and there are layers of food with little
space for my pizza, I feel a little frustrated by this*

*The door of the cafe opens and two obnoxious characters walk in.
They are brothers and recognise me and I vaguely recognise them as
dental patients of mine. One is small and has a walking crutch; he
is the older of the two. The younger one is well built and carrying
heavy dumbbells in his hands. He shouts out to me 'We've been
looking for you!'*

*I attempt to shrug off their advances by replying 'I'm like Freddie
Mercury – I'm the invisible man'*

*I realise that they don't connect with the reference to the song and
I am forced to deal with them*

*The younger brother proceeds into the back room while the older one
nudges up beside me*

*I make small talk with him about his muscle degenerative disease
as I look through a closet of garments for my worktop (a dentist's
scrub). The other brother is now perched on the dental chair and is
awaiting me, I struggle to find the garment and become increasingly
anxious until I awake in my bedroom – it was a dream.*

In an MSE, there are both external and internal aspects of the
patient to be considered. How the patient appears physically and
how he or she portrays himself or herself (e.g. dress sense and
cleanliness) can give us a certain amount of insight. But we are
looking for more prominent expressions, like tics and twitches or
altered gaits. Poor motor skills or an inability to communicate due
to compromised speech can help us paint a picture of the person's
mental aptitude. Features like skin blemishes, bad teeth and track
marks on body parts can indicate drug or alcohol abuse. I pass this
first part of the test by proxy. My sanity has been preserved thus far.

But let's not let me off the hook too easily. We can use other
criteria to examine my dreaming self, so let's begin with *behaviour.*
To shoot someone and casually examine the gun afterwards cannot

be considered normal behaviour. My attempt to kill my friend would certainly constitute an abnormality. I do behave normally in the rest of the dream, but the red flag raised at the outset is cause for alarm as far as my sanity is concerned.

Speech: Although I do not engage in much conversation, I still manage to communicate fluently with a few of my fellow dream beings. I do not recall any impediment to speech and we can infer from the response of my dream peers that I must have expressed myself in a sensible manner. Although the two brothers did not respond to my Queen lyrics, I inferred that this was due to the fact that they did not know the song rather than any misunderstanding of what I said.

Thought content: The dreamscape itself is made of thoughts so we could consider this aspect by looking at the particulars of my dreaming narrative. However, I will adopt a similar stance to Hobson and treat the dreamer and their world as the dreamer does – by examining the dreamer directly and giving the benefit of the doubt to the world that is being experienced. I am aware that my friend feels dishonoured when I shoot him, although I brush it off as something unimportant. This might seem like an abnormal response to attempted murder. My thought process was more focused on the cotton exploding from the vest. The sense of fascination continued when I mused about the weapon after discharging it in the tunnel. We cannot consider this as normal in light of what had just happened.

The thought content remains quite normal after the shooting. I recall my internal response to my friend's arrest; I felt bad for him, which is an empathetic response. Psychopathic minds do not normally demonstrate this kind of response. I should say, however, that this friend of mine neither works at the BBC nor takes intravenous drugs, so my acceptance of the affair as true is in itself cause for concern as I did not recognise the incongruence between truth and fantasy.

I remain grounded when the ticket lady arrives and even have a healthy sense of trepidation about being caught for fare-dodging as well as the possibility of a train crash. These are normal thought processes. I admire the buildings on the hillside and remark to myself how familiar this place is and how I occasionally visit the area. This memory is a false one. I make these assertions to qualify the contents of my dream, but in truth they have no bearing on any real history. I am therefore confabulating in order to rationalise my circumstances.

Despite the fact that I am interacting with what we might describe as hallucinations and telling myself stories in order to string them together, I still maintain a degree of composure. I am able to mentally comment on the thugs' unfamiliarity with the Queen song and navigate my encounter with them in a self-conscious manner. I am mentally capable of recognising that they are trying to intimidate me and I am able to maintain a surface-level conversation with them in order to disguise my unease.

So, in summary, my thought process could be described in any of three different ways. We could say that my thoughts are my reality and that I am interacting with them directly in a hallucinatory form and treating them as real. This would be cause for concern for my mental apparatus. The alternative is to look at the dream as real and then examine the dreamer's thoughts directly. If we take this approach, I get off to a bad start by attempting to kill someone without any real concern as to what this might mean. Otherwise, my thought processes are pretty normal. The third way to consider my thought process is to think of it as a combination of the two. If we do this, then I am delusional as what I perceive to be my reality is not normal.

Perceptions: The clinician will normally seek to determine whether or not the subject is interacting with hallucinations or illusions. Hallucinations are defined as an entirely internal event whereas illusions are distortions of external sensory experience. Again, we are forced to decide what it is that constitutes the dreamer's reality. If we adopt the classical stance that dreams are hallucinations, then I would fail the test.

Thought process: This is not an examination of the content, but rather an appraisal of how the person's mind is operating. This is normally indirectly observed by listening to speech, observing body behaviour, etc. The patient may even reveal something of their thinking by telling us about what is going on in his or her mind but this is not always reliable. In the case of my dream, we have direct access to the contents of my mind, so we can see how rapidly the narrative changes and how incongruent the themes are in relation to each other. An example is how the café becomes a waiting room for a dentist. We call this kind of flitting from one subject to another *knight's move thinking*.

My thought process is constantly being derailed as my narrative runs through a number of different scenarios, which are only loosely associated with each other. The transitions are inconsistent; I step off the train into the café without going through the anticipated train station. My casual attempt to kill someone skips onto an encounter centred on my train ticket and then to an awkward experience with a couple of thugs. One would think that a killer would not be so easily intimidated by the young lady or even the brothers and yet I was. This incongruence in both my personality and my thinking is evidence of an erratic thought process, which suggests mental incompetence.

Mood and affect: The mood of the patient is evident in how they express their feelings to the physician, whereas the affect is what the clinician observes and deduces about the person's mood. In this regard, I would say that I was emotionally detached. The remorse I might have felt for shooting my friend was quickly superseded by an overwhelming sense of curiosity about the gun, followed by contemplation of the sound of the silencer in the tunnel. I paid no attention to the ticket inspector after I discharged the weapon. It did not cross my mind that I might get in trouble for shooting a live firearm in a public place. This laissez-faire attitude suggests that I had insulated myself from the consequences of my actions and did not engage in any emotional response, despite the gravity of my situation.

I show a more normal response when I become aware that my ticket might not be valid. I also display a self-preservation instinct when I am intimidated by the brothers, but I think it is fair to suggest that my mood is that of someone who is not emoting normally and that my lack of ability to consider my actions empathically indicates a compromised mood. At no point was I depressed or anxious. No extreme emotion was observed. *A hyper-emotional state would be indicative of schizophrenic behaviour whereas dulled emotion would be more consistent with mental deficiency syndrome* – this reiterates Hobson's remark about Delia and her equivalent state when he evaluated her.

Cognition: Cognitive faculties would normally be tested using specific tests in order to determine attention, orientation, alertness and memory, but we cannot test the subject in this situation. However, what we can say is that I am disoriented as the dream begins as I don't know how I ended up at that place. I am on a random train whose destination I do not know. It is only when I look out the windows that I comment on how much I like to visit this place, implying familiarity. But there is no way I could be recalling the area as I have never actually been there, so I am relying on a false memory to iron out the creases in my story. I exhibit a similar type of mental accommodation when I meet the thuggish brothers. I acknowledge their recognition of me and vaguely recognise them too. In hindsight, I do not know these characters at all and so must conclude that any memory I had of them at the time was confabulated.

Short-term memory and attention were lacking as I had dismissed the attempted murder by the time the ticket lady arrived. All I felt was a superficial concern for my own social safety. My inattention was evident as I quickly lost interest even in this and allowed myself to get caught up in the view of the cartoon-like buildings on the hillside. My attention was then drawn to the train tracks and their chaotic layout. This is all evidence of the total abandonment of my cognitive functioning.

Judgement: I cannot say much in defence of my attempted murder except that I did not see anything wrong with what I had just done. It was only the look of disgust on my friend's face that prompted any sense of remorse, but this was quickly eclipsed by my fascination with the cocking action of the gun. This demonstrates a total lack of insight of how I should behave. I must also remark that I did not give any consideration to the consequences of shooting my friend before acting. My inability to plan and execute tasks accordingly suggests that my executive function was offline. I do not show signs of sufficient reasoning and must be regarded as having severely impaired judgement.

Insight: This is something that would require the patient to comment on how they feel about their condition, but I cannot offer any such remark as I am completely immersed in mine. However, it is not knowing that I am dreaming that causes me to behave the way that I do. It is because I lack the self-reflective sense of being that normally guides my waking-world feelings and decisions that I have lack insight. The dreaming mind does not facilitate adequate intellectual insight about our actions and so I fail this test too.

In conclusion, we have demonstrated that the dreaming mind meets the criteria for a kind of natural nocturnal dementia. If we were to behave in the waking world as we do in dreams, we would find it very difficult to comprehend reality at all. The lucid dreamer, I postulated, is straggled between the insanity of the dream and the rationality of the waking mind. It is here, I anticipated, beyond the horizon of conventional scientific orthodoxy that the method could be harvested from madness. And thus it was in the exotic landscape of the lucid dream, so fertile with ideological flexibility, that I eventually discovered the reason why we lose ourselves for so many hours on any given night and what this could tell us about our puzzling picture of consciousness ...

7) Enter the Shaman

To illustrate my own examination of acute nocturnal psychosis I will pick up where Hobson left off, with his suggestion that there might be a connection between the dreaming brain and schizophrenia. He is careful to point out that the schizophrenic exhibits an acute emotional response, which is not normally seen in the dreaming brain. The classic paranoid and/or manic behaviour associated with schizophrenia is not usually observed in the dreaming self, so the diagnosis falls short, but only just. I want to see if I can bridge this gap with my own vision of altered states of consciousness.

Hobson divides his model of consciousness into three primary states – waking, sleeping and dreaming. He alludes to the possibility of hybrid states whereby the dreaming state may leak into the waking state or vice versa, causing a variety of conditions. The lucid dream is not considered one of his primary states as he does not yet feel we enter this state with sufficient frequency. I agree with this point of view, although I expect we will gradually see more people entering this state through practice and increased technological help in the future.

There is already evidence that social etiquette can influence states of consciousness. In some cultures dreaming is an essential part of culture. I am not just speaking about the tribal folk that we might normally associate with such practices. More contemporary movements such as Buddhism also take an active approach to dreaming. My friend Charlie Morley, who is a practising Tibetan Buddhist, tells me that dream yoga, which he teaches all around the world, is considered to be a sophisticated form of meditation that one can use to understand the nature of reality and eventually reach enlightenment. He discusses this in detail in 'Dreams of Awakening', in which he outlines lucid dreaming as an authenticated spiritual practice.

I adamantly encourage this kind of *cross-cultural fertilisation* – that is, taking on each other's ideas and seeing them in a new light. This is what McKenna and Leary envisioned when they encountered the internet in its infancy. They could see what would emerge from this embryo: a super global mind that could interact with itself and reach its full potential through a hyper-technical feedback mechanism. Nowadays this is made manifest on Twitter, YouTube or Google. How the inter-mind will look is impossible to envision, but I am proposing that the fertilisation has already taken place and that the foetus is beginning to take form online.

In a world that is fuelled by information, one of the fundamental merits of technology is communication. We are finally able to consider each everyone's point of view, regardless of whom or where any given person is. Our model of reality must bend to accommodate the view of the other as we are forced to face the possibility that what we have known until now may be nothing more than our own limited software program. Perhaps the Hindus have something to tell us, maybe the Senoi tribe in Malaysia do. There are countless cultural operating systems for us to explore and try on for size, but none should be considered complete in its own right, not even our own model of physics. Our scientific view is successful at producing technology, but it has caused us to push nature to the brink of destruction with our careless consumption of resources. On the contrary, the 'primitive' natives of America had great respect for the land and success cultivating it until we came along. Perhaps they had a more sophisticated understanding of how the world works than we do today.

McKenna was a firm advocate of this view. He alluded to himself as an activist for the preservation of nature, although he specifically referred himself as a shamanologist, a term he used to describe somebody who studied the work of shamans. *A shaman is a person who learns how to enter altered states of consciousness in order to interact with the spiritual world and channel its power into ours with the intention of helping, healing and guiding his or her community.* Typically practised in non-Western cultures, the job of the shaman, according to McKenna, is to heal the sick, predict the weather and tell hunters where the best game is likely to be found. He or she may also act as an adjudicator when dealing with crimes that have been committed in the community, using his or her powers to time travel and witness the event. Doctors and scientists perform similar duties in the West, but our heritage is classically monophasic, and we should not assume that we know any better but instead understand that we just see the world differently.

Our society views mental health in a way that stands in complete opposition to that of the shamanic tribes. In our world, people who hallucinate are deemed mentally unwell. They are frequently diagnosed with some form of dementia and are marginalised by the community. The shaman, by contrast, is the healer of the tribe. It is strange that the shaman is often chosen because of his/her ability to hallucinate. This mental 'deficiency' separates the potential shaman from the rest to the tribe. What we call a disease, the aboriginal peoples call a gift and what we call a maniac, they call a healer.

It is important point to understand how radically different our perspectives of reality can be and yet each can be substantiated in its own right. When we are willing to work holistically, we can start to put the pieces of the jigsaw of consciousness together. I look, as an example, at Hobson's model of dreaming. He posits a possible connection between schizophrenia and dreaming but stops short of describing them as identical because one thing is lacking: the acute emotional activity we normally associate with schizoid attacks. But McKenna could see the connection. He writes that, 'A shaman is someone who swims in the same ocean as the schizophrenic, but the shaman has thousands and thousands of years of sanctioned technique and tradition to draw upon.'

McKenna identified what he refers to as *shamanic ecstasy*, which is the eruption of emotion when the shaman enters into a trance. It might seem like manic behaviour to us, but to the shaman it is a connection with the divine. The shaman would normally be intoxicated by the psychedelic plants or exhaustion from drumming, singing and/or dancing. McKenna is careful to point out the difference between the two approaches here, citing the use of plants as the more authentic of the forms of intoxication. He tells us that once the use of plants has been dropped from the ceremony, the ritual is heading towards religion.

Dreaming is also the duty of the shamanic elder. He may enter Hobson's hybrid state of dreaming/waking. He can maintain a degree of intellectual balance, avoiding some of the more traumatic side effects associated with dreaming, such as disorientation, lack of insight, judgement and diminished cognitive function. One might call the shaman a lucid dreamer. Indeed, lucid dreamers all around the world are becoming increasingly curious about the ability of lucid dreaming to heal. My friend Caroline McCready joins Robert Waggoner to discuss this in vivid detail in their book – Lucid Dreaming, Plain and Simple. They offer some very intriguing examples as well as an outline of some techniques that may be applied by the budding dream worker. Perhaps lucid dreamers will take on a more shamanic role in years to come.

The connection between psychedelic plants and lucid dreaming has been a tenuous one until now. As somebody who has a relationship with both, I can see the connection but there seems to be a common misunderstanding about the use of plants. Some people naively suggest that the plant is a shortcut to spirituality. Nothing could be further from the truth. Taking psychedelic substances is an art in its own right. One must have great mental strength and every experience is so different that the idea of reaching any spiritual or intellectual end goal seems like an oxymoron. Nothing could prepare a person for the total wonder induced by such substances. It is indescribable. For this reason, it is crucial to take the correct dose in appropriate surroundings under supervision, with the correct mind-set.

The shaman's role is to hold the space as he/she takes you into his/her world, acting as a guide. It is his/her voice that you come to when you feel lost for it is he/she who knows how to navigate the netherworlds of the mind. Like lost sheep we can listen to his/her bell when the storm of consciousness gets too rough in the throes of the ecstatic trip we have undertaken.

One simply cannot underestimate the potential of the plant. The people of the Amazon do not have a word for 'drug'. It is our subversion of language that consigns these agents of healing and knowledge to the realm of the dirty and dangerous. The cultural propaganda that pervades our society does not always help you learn; it can just as easily prevent one from attaining a higher level of consciousness and often only serves the authority figures whose purpose it is to keep the world ignorant in order to sustain their dominance.

Modern-Day Shamanism

Psychedelics have been exiled from our society. This is the case not only for the 'recreational use' of such drugs, but also for medical treatment. In the US and the UK, they are *legally classified as having no scientific merit or medical use whatsoever*. We have only come into contact with these substances in the last 100 years or so and already we are being forced to close our account on the subject. We are told this is because they are dangerous and of no practical use, but how can such a conclusion be reached if we have not yet researched them adequately. There was a brief window between their discovery and their prohibition about fifty years ago, during which time there was an indication that they could help manage a variety of mental disorders, including depression, addiction and PTSD.

Thankfully, research charities like the wonderful MAPS (Multidisciplinary Association for Psychedelic Studies) and The Heffter Research Institute as well as mavericks like Professor David Nutt are making headlines with their research into the possible uses and benefits of these substances. I don't think it would be unjust to refer to these people and institutions as important players in the modern-day shamanic movement.

In my search for Factor X, plants would eventually play a part. It was not, however, the psychedelic variety that proved to be the key but a plant that had the opposite effect. I recall sitting on a panel at the annual Gateways of the Mind Conference in London in 2012. My peer Professor Nutt had just been fired by our own government for his statistical analysis of drug danger. He had concluded that legal drugs like alcohol were of much more concern than non-addictive drugs like ecstasy. He was bucking the trend by telling us that ecstasy's active ingredient MDMA (3,4-methylenedioxy-N methylamphetamine) was not only non-addictive but that it could also be an effective treatment for depression and anxiety disorders.

For the first time in medical history, we had a picture of the brain under the influence of a psychedelic. We had anticipated a neurological firework display but what we got was less like 4 July and more like 4 January. Aldous Huxley, inspired by his experience with peyote, gave an account of what the drug was like in his novel *The Doors of Perception*, in which he defines the brain as a kind of reduction valve. He suggests that the duty of the brain is to restrict the flow of information and that taking psychedelics allows the valve to be temporarily loosened so more information can be taken on by the person. This was eventually validated when we scanned the psychedelic brain.

We observed a dulling down of certain cerebral components, specifically the medial prefrontal cortex (mPFC) and the posterior cingulate cortex (PCC). These two areas appear to play important roles in the regulation of self-awareness. They are particularly active when people are asked to think about themselves, for example.

These brain parts form an area collectively referred to as the *default mode network*, which is most active when we are introspecting and not goal-focused. This wandering of the mind is a common symptom of depression. One withdraws from the outside world and over-invests in the self. Psychiatrists think this over-inflated sense of self may be the cause of the condition.

The psychedelic dissolves this rigid view of reality by loosening the patient's overly tightened psychological reduction valve. This dulls the person's sense of self, allowing a specially trained counsellor to enter into therapy with the patient with a view of unravelling deep psychological stresses, which would otherwise be inaccessible because the ego's defence mechanism normally guards our inner thoughts and feelings. Dr Rick Doblin of MAPS, a pioneer of this course of treatment, says that they are making incredible progress with soldiers suffering from PTSD. It is early days, but the clinical trials and the scientific essays are stacking up and pressure is building for governments to reclassify the substances for medicinal use. The US army has invested heavily in this research. This support is sure to have a significant impact on the future of such 'drugs'.

The aim should be to decriminalise these mind altering agents eventually, so they can be used not just for medicinal purposes, but also for more abstract processes like creative thinking. In *Island* Aldous Huxley imagines a utopia where psychedelics are taken to help society to develop in a more altruistic manner. The story tells of a sacred mushroom that must be consumed as a rite of passage by every 18-year-old on the island to help them to integrate into a more balanced society. He clearly recognised the shaman's role as a healer and could see the potential for these powerful gifts from nature.

The Gateways of the Mind conference panel of 2012, in London, consisted mostly of lucid dream experts. I was there as a plant enthusiast. I had just heard the news from Professor Nutt and his team and had not yet made the connection between plants and lucid dreaming. Coincidentally, in the same year, a team of scientists who had taken an interest in observing the brain activity of lucid dreamers identified what happens to the brain the moment the light of lucidity is switched on in the dreamer's mind.

The Max Planck Institute in Germany has become synonymous with lucid dreaming. It was their ground-breaking imaging research that first revealed what might one day prove to be the seat of self-conscious awareness. The principle is simple. They took people who had the ability to lucid dream and connected them to monitors in the same way LaBerge and Hearne had many years before, but with the addition of functional magnetic resonance imaging technology. It proved possible to see the shifts in brain activity when the subjects fell asleep, when they began dreaming and, most importantly, the moment when they became aware that they were dreaming.

According to Michael Czisch of the institute, they saw that, 'in a lucid state the activity in certain areas of the cerebral cortex increases markedly within seconds. The involved areas of the cerebral cortex are the right dorsolateral prefrontal cortex, to which commonly the function of self-assessment is attributed, and the frontopolar regions, which are responsible for evaluating our own thoughts and feelings. The precuneus is also especially active, a part of the brain that has long been linked with self-perception.' So the sense of self is not being dulled but amplified!

Closing In On Factor X

Putting the two halves of this equation together, what we see emerging is a kind of toggle switch that allows the person to move from ordinary states of reality to the mystical or magic end of the spectrum. It was apparent to me that what we were looking at was the mind's ability to enter states in which the dimensions of space and time give way and reality becomes a place where the observer can interact with creations of their own imagination. The scanning technology we are only beginning to utilise indicated that the default mode network was the key area of this cerebral activity. This was the case for both the lucid dream and the psychedelic process.

What I now envisioned was a spectrum of consciousness that would allow one to start at either end and move towards the other. The dreamer who was not self-aware could become lucid and we also know sufficiently high doses of psychedelics diminished the ego's sense of self to such a degree that the person loses any sense of who they are, allowing the mind to enter severely altered states of being. It still needed to be demonstrated that this was not a kind of trick of the mind, but something far more significant. It was my belief that our cultural myopia had prevented us from seeing the true value of these states, which 'primitive' peoples consider a gift.

What I propose is something like a volume switch, which could be toggled from a critically self-aware state of consciousness to a diminished-self state of consciousness which I refer to as pre-critical. The latter state, I anticipated, would not require the narrative feedback mechanism the critical observer would ordinarily need to make sense of the world. It is because we have a congruent story about our world that we can talk about the idea of reality at all. For this to be possible we need to have a history feeding our present. The dreaming or magic state would not require this to the same degree because the observer lacks a sense of their own being. It was this shift from the critical to the pre-critical observer that would determine the type of physics needed, be it classical or quantum, the latter allowing for retro-causality and hence flagrant psychological confabulation to ensue.

If I was correct, then I would expect to see a direct correlation between our sense of self and the nature of the world we occupy. My push-ups test demonstrated that it was possible to feel as light as a balloon and as heavy as lead, but it also showed that there is a middle ground: I was able to sustain a sense of limitless strength and stamina. It was this middle state that led me to contemplate the matter further. Were we witnessing the perfect symmetry of body and mind? I feel that when we become lucid, the dream starts to reflect this in its physical behaviour. I anticipate that the more lucidly aware we are the denser and more narratively congruent the dream becomes as the more classical type of matter form takes hold.

The physicist in me extrapolates that what we may be looking at here is a thermodynamic relationship whereby the level of organisation of the system is tantamount to the level of energy present. The more highly organised a system is, the more energy it requires to sustain it. As an example – your body needs food for energy and this energy, in turn, keeps you from falling apart by sustaining your tissue structure. Likewise the more lucid and logical our mind becomes, the more energy it too would need to be stable.

Not to risk covering ourselves in chalk at the proverbial blackboard, but if we really want to be thorough here we must briefly ask what those letters in Einstein's notorious E=MC2 equation actually mean. I certainly won't go into too much detail here, suffice to say that (E)nergy =(M)ass, which is to say that the two are equivalent. The more energy a system has the more mass it holds.

This, I postulate, should equate to more weight and hence the push-ups should become more difficult as we progress into more lucid states of consciousness. Thus we have a gradient of mass which would be parallel to our level of self-reflective awareness. This would certainly satisfy the results from my experiment if we could measure an equivalent correspondence between my perceived weight and my intellectual acuity at the time.

Although the specifics of the physics might be a little controversial here I cannot help but to feel that the argument does hold some sway and it certainly marries up to our axiom that dreams are made of atoms. Whether one agrees or not with this deeper aspect of the theory, we may still be able to construe a relationship between the state of organisation of the self and the particular expression of the ensuing physics. I visualise this as a lens, through which we can direct our attention. If we direct it at the lens from one side, our awareness is constricted into a narrow sense of being and if we direct it from the other side, it spreads out, resulting in an expanded sense of perception. We could direct our attention at the lens from both sides at the same time. Our state of consciousness would then be determined by where the lens sits. If it slides towards one source, we get the narrow beam effect, which represents the egoistic or problem-solving mind, and if we slide it towards the other, we get the wider beam, which represents the diminished sense of self or the dreaming mind.

This constricting and expanding of consciousness is exhibited by both lucid dreaming and psychedelic brain scanning studies. Both point to the same basic principle: self-critical awareness is increased or decreased during each process. Both the psychedelic and the ordinary dream state offer us a world that exhibits the qualities of quantum weirdness because both are characterised by time distortion, a lack of distinct causality, a disruption of locality and a dilution of mass. It is important to remember that both of these states involve a diminished sense of self.

In dreams our reality can assume many different appearances as the sense of self-reflective awareness is severely diminished. Likewise we can say that the degree to which one can experience magic with psychedelics is dependent on the amount consumed and so how diluted one's sense of self is. A low dose will make the person feel elated and giddy, with mild hallucinations. Moderate doses will cause the person to feel disoriented and confused, with an increase in hallucinations and possibly a shift from purely visual effects to auditory activity as well; the person may suffer from paranoia or, in some cases, ecstasy. On a full or 'heroic' dose, one can feel completely obliterated, with auditory, visual and even kinaesthetic hallucinations. Other beings can enter the space and communicate, offering advice and insight. The experience can take the individual to a different world, in which the 'rules' of reality no longer apply.

The less self-critically aware one allows oneself to become, the more absurd the trip becomes. But there is something one should consider before taking such a trip – the psychedelic agent does not have an off button. Sometimes this causes a retaliation of the ego, which senses that it is being annihilated. One feels like they are going to die or, worse, lose one's mind. This latter effect can occur because when there is no self, there is no familiar point of reference from which to measure our world.

When we are more critically self-aware, our minds act in a more conventionally logical way, but it is this very rationality that demands causality and order in the world, thus lessening the magic element of the experience. Psychedelics give us a clear illustration of this inverse relationship between self-awareness and magic. We find a similar pattern with lucid dreaming. Lucid dreaming, like psychedelic consciousness, is not a binary affair of lucid or non-lucid, but a bandwidth of awareness that varies from mild lucidity to being critically aware enough to recite Shakespeare from your school years.

I now refer to this conceptual description as *the double-edge self-theory*, and in summary it holds that **the more critically self-aware we become, the more rigidly reality behaves** or to put that another way **magical states are inversely proportional to self-reflective awareness**. Taking psychedelics or meditating diminishes the organisation of the ego and allows us to enter transcendental states. Dreaming is also a diminished-ego state, but the sense of self kicks in when we become lucid. Although the dream retains some of its quantum-like features, it tends to change its texture and behaves more rationally and rigidly. One might say that we are looking at a reciprocal relationship between magic and critical self-awareness.

Our self-image in dreams fits with this idea. When we look at mirrors in lucid dreams, we can see a wide range of reflections. They can vary from ordinary likenesses to no reflection at all and just about anything in between. One could infer from the reflection observed the level of association between the dreamer and what they perceive to be his or her ordinary self. The more depreciated the self-concept has become, the less we associate the ordinary sense of self with the dreamer and the more distorted the image in the mirror is likely to be.

Rise of the Dream Warrior

I contemplated self-image in lucid dreams and how actively abandoning my default sense of self might imbue me with power. My theory was simple – the less I held onto my normal self, the less critically conscious I would be and hence the more magic I would be capable of in the dream state. With this in mind, I decided to fashion a character for myself in the inner world: a mystical warrior with a superhero-like image and the ability to transgress the boundaries of space and time.

On the night my new dream self was created I stood in front of a mirror in my dream bedroom, fully lucid and yet detached. I willed my clothes to turn black. To my amazement, it worked. I reached over my right shoulder, willing there to be a samurai sword strapped to my back – and there it was. I gripped the sword and unsheathed it. I looked at its incredible Japanese craftsmanship. It was beautifully engraved with a variety of Asian symbols. I went off into the night. The Dream Warrior was born …

Now that I had established my second life in the dream world, I wanted to share this discovery about the nature of our world, so I set up my own website, www.wakeupinyourdreams.com. The tagline from the outset was 'What is Reality..?' In hindsight, the operation was meant as a beacon to see if anybody else was experiencing the kind of thing I was experimenting with. I know that my site has attracted others on this same quest and it has helped me to forge alliances with people who have come to a similar understanding of how our world is evolving.

'Dream Warrior' became the name I was known by and the operation snowballed into quite a little social enterprise.

I appeared on the cover of the magazine that I had grown up reading, *Martial Arts Illustrated*. The editor, Bob Sykes, now a good friend and a fellow practitioner of altered states of consciousness, tells me that he came up with the idea for the magazine in 1987, which was also the year I had travelled back to in order to meet my younger self. The magazine was first printed in 1988. Could this be a coincidence? I guess that depends on your view of reality ...

Carl Jung wrote about synchronicity, whereby an apparent coincidence can have a deeper meaning, which is invisible to us on this layer of reality. This is reminiscent of quantum entanglement tying events together. In dreaming, for example, we are aware of hyper-association, i.e. how the mind links events by meaning and jumps from idea to idea accordingly. In the case of my recorded dream above, I might have associated the attempted murder with getting caught by the ticket inspector, which I might have associated with punishment, which was represented by the thugs. We can easily see patterns like this in dreams, but do not normally make such associations between events that occur in the waking world. By neglecting to do so, we adopt the stance that matter is indifferent to meaning and that in the physical world the significance of loosely related events does not warrant attention.

However, people who regularly dissolve the ego, through practices like meditation or the use of psychedelic substances, lean towards the more entangled, synchronistic view of reality. They say that everything is connected on a more subtle level than we normally perceive and that this becomes more apparent when we open up to it. Perhaps the diminished-ego state of consciousness allows one to see more synchronicity in the world. This would certainly fit our double-edge self-model. Perhaps there are no coincidences, but only deep, hidden relationships, the likes of which Einstein felt uneasy about. P.W. Bridgeman, a philosopher of science, humorously defined a coincidence as what you have left over when you apply a bad theory.

Whatever about coincidences, the internet makes everybody and everything feel closer. It seems as if one could connect with any individual or idea at any time. It is an unparalleled forum for discussion. I frequently receive emails from other curious souls, people who are asking the same questions about this strange world as I am. It feels like we are building an online army of people who want to reconsider our perception of reality.

My Dream Warrior became more than an ego trip for me. It meant something to the people who came on to my site and agreed with my views. The character became a light in the darkness, something that prompted people to wonder if it was possible to live as a dual-identity superhero – I was a dentist by day and a samurai-slashing warrior who could transcend space and time at night. But I had become something greater than all that. My being had revealed its true nature. I was no longer a biological bag of skin and bones, grinding out meaningless, meandering memories. A vision had emerged from the space between the thoughts – 'I' had become an idea …

The Paradox of Lucid Dreaming

8) The Red Pill

My theory was not complete as I could not yet find a deeper link between the biology and the physics. I was looking for something transcendental, something both tangible and intangible, like the mathematics that holds our world together. We cannot physically touch an equation and yet it acts as the glue of our world. I thought my Factor X might have a similar quality to it, that it too could be abstract and invisible and yet evident all around us. I likened it to the water in fishbowl. Imagine asking a fish what water was. Perhaps they do not notice it all, even though they are constantly immersed in it.

I decided to work with what I had – a model of reality that suggested a spectrum of states, ranging from the well-behaved, causal states to the other end of the scale, where uncertainty and probability prevailed. At this latter end of the scale, time was not strict and matter was difficult to define without resorting to paradoxical frames of reference. This model of reality held that reality was determined by us, the observers. It seemed to me that reality was constituted based on the state of the observer – a constricted critical view made the world solid and time-focussed whereas an expanded view, with a dulled sense of self, would result in a more flexible reality where causality could go in either direction, if at all.

If my model was to stand up, I had to look at the potential holes in the argument. There was one in particular – the state of sleep. When we talk about lucid dreaming, we normally refer to a dream during which one notices that one is dreaming and so engages the pre-frontal cortex, allowing a self-reflective negotiation of the world. However, as dreaming tends to occur primarily at the end of the sleep cycle, we end up with occasional brief periods of complete unconsciousness each day. Although this gap in our reality state does not contradict our model, it does make it less elegant. But as I discovered, it is possible to iron out the creases and show a continuity of consciousness, whereby the lucid dream can be entered and exited seamlessly from and to the waking state.

The brain operates with a daily cycle mechanism. We go from waking to sleeping, then on to dreaming until waking again. Normally we undergo four to five sleep cycles a night, each one approximately ninety minutes long. During each cycle, there are four stages of sleep, starting with the lightest and progressing towards the deepest before re-cycling back to the lighter end again. There is a progressive slowing-down of brainwave function from about 10Hz (stage 1) to 4Hz (stage 4). The figures and details vary but the basic process remains constant: a gradual loosening of attentive awareness and an eventual loss of consciousness. At stage 4, we are in deep sleep and brain activity is minimised. Dreaming is not commonly reported at this stage.

After stage 4, the brain goes back to faster wave states, climbing back through stages 3, 2 and 1 until it enters a different kind of sleep, known as REM. During REM sleep, brainwave activity is close to that of the waking state. However, it is harder to rouse the subject from this state than any other. Waking normally occurs after REM sleep, at the end of the ninety-minute cycle. There is a brief period of wakefulness before the sleeper returns to stage 1 sleep to repeat the cycle. Alternatively the person remains awake.

Dreaming usually occurs during REM sleep. However, the classic audio-visual display of REM is not the only type of dream we can experience. It is possible to experience dream activity in deeper states of sleep, but we do not often notice or remember these. We are capable of remembering REM dreams, but our memory of dreams decays rapidly after waking. The window period between waking and forgetting the dream allows for a brief period of reflection and people who keep dream diaries use this time to record the night's dreams.

The Thin Red Line

The transition from dreaming to waking is not always something we are conscious of. Even when we are, we quickly forget it. But sometimes we do notice the transaction. This is usually observed in one of three ways.

We can transition instantly from dreaming to waking. This is probably the most common and familiar transition. We are not usually critically aware of the dream at the time and can only refer to it in retrospect. We feel an instantaneous shift in consciousness, i.e. we go from dreaming to waking smoothly, without the sense of a hiatus. This is qualified by laboratory observation, which has shown that the shift occurs in an instant.

The second type of transition involves interference from the waking world, such as a knock on the door, which is then drawn into the dream and incorporated into the narrative before causing the person to wake up. The knock on the door might cause the person to hear a gun being fired as the confabulating, hyper-associative brain might be able to hallucinate such an event to accommodate the interference. One does not always wake up after such an intrusion. Lucid dreamers have even managed to take advantage of such intrusions by developing technology to help them induce lucid dreams.

It was Stephen LaBerge who first commercially utilised the dreaming brain's habit of incorporating external stimuli to trigger lucid dreams. He initially created the Dream Light, later refined and renamed the Novadreamer, an eye mask which detects REM sleep and responds by illuminating a red LED light display resting against the dreamer's eyes. These lights are just strong enough to send a signal through the eyelid and along the optic nerve to the visual cortex of the dreamer. In the same way the auditory cortex can incorporate external input (e.g. the knocking on the door); the visual cortex can incorporate incoming light signals into the dream. A light signal appears in the dream narrative. We can recognise this signal and become lucid. There have been subsequent versions of this mask, including Aurora by iWinks, which have turned it into a more comfortable headband to wear. They all act on the same principle.

The technique works, but it is not as simple as it sounds. One can be over-stimulated by the apparatus or even under-stimulated, in which case one does not notice the lights at all. Even when the dreamer does notice the lights, the mind often retrofits a narrative onto it so it makes sense in the context of the dream. As an example, I once used a light-induction device. In my dream, I was hanging out with friends at my old school when the REM Dreamer machine (a similar product to the Novadreamer) set off the light cues. I recall the sky filling up with a firework display, which eventually ended with the words, 'Disney's Lilo and Stitch'. I turned to my friend and said, 'Disney must have spent a fortune on that.' It was not until the next morning that I realised what had actually happened: the dream had fashioned the light cue into a light-based dream event. This highlights how difficult it can be for lucidity to penetrate dreams; the mind is so capable of disguising itself from itself.

The third type of transition is exclusive to lucid dreamers. We can decide that we want to wake up from the dream and remain aware throughout this process to observe it. Waking from a lucid dream gives us a peek into the transition process. It tends to resemble the transition from a normal dream to waking. However, I recall once hearing the alarm clock in my bedroom when I was in a lucid dream. As I was lucid, it wasn't disguised or incorporated. I recognised it as my alarm, yet I did not wake up for a couple of minutes. I recall the sound filling the dream air as I turned to the other dream beings I was with and informed them that my alarm was ringing, so I needed to get up and go to work. I waved them goodbye and decided to wake up.

Even today, I find that story intriguing. I was able to subdue the sound so as not to wake myself. Waking up was my choice, despite the intrusion of the alarm. This goes to show just how thin the line between waking and dreaming is. One moment we can be falling to our death and the next we can sitting upright our beds. If we take this at face value, it's difficult not to feel a little crazy. This shift may not be too unlike what Hobson tells us about the nature of consciousness. We can imagine our critical functioning jumping from the pre-reflective to the reflective state, causing the wave function to collapse and reality to solidify. The mentally compromised individual, I speculate, may lack the mechanism to control the critical function appropriately, with the result that one leg remains stuck in the dreaming reality as they fail to fully transition and this quantum state of reality overspills into their ordinary state of being.

I think my model holds water, but as I have already mentioned, I was troubled by the fact that consciousness could temporarily black-out between waking and dreaming. I was forced to lose sight of the observer for a brief period when attempting to initiate a lucid dream. This meant that it wasn't strictly a first-hand analysis of the process as a whole. The only solution for such a problem would be to enter from the waking state directly into a lucid dream and thankfully Stepahen La Berge had already mapped out this territory for me.

LaBerge is still considered by many to be the leading researcher in the field of lucid dreaming. Much of his terminology is still used in discussions of the subject today. He is a pragmatic individual and is careful not to offer too mystical an explanation for what he does. Publicly, he tries to remain within the current scientific status quo as much as possible.

I cannot pretend to do the same but I do at least try to remain rationalist. I agree that extraordinary claims require extraordinary proof, even if it is the proof of one's own experience. As a lucid dreamer, I know that it is easy to come ungrounded in your thinking – after all, you are entering the world of magic, but even magic has its boundaries. It is important to avoid, as much as possible, confusing anecdote for fact in our discussion.

Out-of-Body Experience

One of the most controversial subjects in the field of altered realities is the out-of-body experience (OBE), not only because of the claim that part of the individual has left his or her body, but also because people who have had such experiences claim to be able to observe the world from outside their bodies during their OBEs. Does this fit with my model of reality? On some level it does, at least in principle. I view it akin to reverse schizophrenia; the primary state of consciousness in this case is in the quantum world and it is the ordinary world that is bleeding into it. With schizophrenia, I speculate the opposite: the quantum world leaks into the ordinary world. Let's examine this idea further before we reach any conclusions.

If we return to the alarm clock situation, in which I was able to temporarily hold consciousness between the two states, we might observe some parallels: in both, consciousness can be held in a semi-collapsed, quasi super-state, with our awareness being broadcasted over the entire operation. One might wonder how the critical function, which is ordinarily fashioned by the brain, might slip out of gear, allowing the person's reality to be plunged into a hybrid state of quantum data superimposed onto the ordinary.

As an example, the brain's reaction to acute trauma or shock is often to go into complete sensory shutdown. However, in some circumstances this mechanism may not function perfectly and so allow a certain amount of awareness to override the system. The person may still have some perception of what is happening to the body and this, I speculate, might result in a decoupling of the sense of self from the body. One might postulate a psychological defence mechanism whereby the critical functioning rejects the traumatised body in an attempt to distance the mind from it. A secondary body would be created by the mind to accommodate the scenario. People do *experience* the sensation of leaving their bodies but do they actually leave their bodies?

To answer this, we must know whether or not we are occupying our bodies at all. As this is unquantifiable, we are left once more with the riddle I presented in the first chapter when I asked if we were a mind experiencing a body or a body experiencing a mind. To articulate ourselves as either would be to place an arbitrary boundary around something we cannot actually define. Therefore we need to look at other aspects of the out-of-body experience to decide how to fit it into our theory of reality.

I am drawn to the OBE because one can enter it from a waking state. It is even possible to induce an OBE with proper training. This presents us with the opportunity to close the gap in my model if we adopt the position that the OBE can be considered a kind of lucid dream. If so, we would be entering the lucid dream directly and thus preserving our continuity of consciousness when transitioning from the waking state to altered state and back again. LaBerge supports this model. He distinguishes two types of lucid dreams – the dream-induced lucid dream (DILD) and the wake-induced lucid dream (WILD). It is the latter that he likens to the OBE. He even suggests that the sensation of leaving the body can be accommodated by the WILD.

I propose, at this stage, substituting the terms DILD and WILD with indirect and direct transitions respectively. These do not commit us to the idea of leaving the body in some form, but only to the idea that we can shift our state of consciousness in a direct or indirect fashion. Likewise, we are not defining the state as a 'dream' either as this could imply an entirely subjective experience to many people. What is crucial to consider here is whether or not it is possible for the secondary body to perceive the waking world directly and comment on matters of a consensual nature.

There are many stories of people leaving their bodies and being nonetheless fully aware of their surroundings once outside the body. Patients have reported witnessing surgeons working on their bodies and soldiers have reported seeing their bodies being tortured while their consciousness was detached above and aware. However, LaBerge argues that what is projected is an image of the body created by the dreaming mind, a counterfeit copy which seems so similar that it is almost impossible to distinguish it and one's real body. He is adamant that the world being observed during the OBE is a replica of the physical plane and not the real world as we ordinarily define it.

He hypothesises that the waking consciousness slips into a lucid dream without the normal interval of sleep (WILD). He believes that the dreaming brain simulates a scenario that resembles that in which the transition is takes place. When I have direct transitions, it is invariably in my bedroom, usually in the early morning. Once the transition concludes, I often find myself in the same bedroom in the dark of night and sometimes I can even see my 'body' lying in bed, asleep. The environment is usually solid to touch and lacks that familiar sense of low gravity that I often experience during the indirect lucid dream transition. It very much resembles the ordinary world, so I can see how easy it would be to think that one is, in fact, observing the ordinary world.

However, it is possible for the dreaming mind to create a world that acts in this way. With the indirect transition, we know that the critical function is switched off temporarily prior to re-engaging. Conversely with the direct transition we must speculate that it is preserved. One would expect to witness a dream state but the world behaves like the ordinary critical state of reality, as opposed to the pre-critical quantum affair that we would normally witness with the indirect transition.

Qualitatively speaking, LaBerge does not see any difference between the OBE and his WILD, other than the idea that someone could leave his or her body and visit a 'target site', i.e. a place where one can go to retrieve information that would otherwise be unknown to them. For example, some trauma patients who have a near-death experience (NDE) report being able leaving their bodies and describe things that might ordinarily be unperceivable for their subdued sensory functions. Some give detailed accounts of the medical care team, including trivial matters like what the various team members were wearing, despite having spent the time lying flat on their backs with their eyes closed and their bodies apparently unconscious.

This idea of being able to view something from a non-local perspective is not exclusive to OBEs. Psychics and remote viewers have long claimed to be able to project their awareness to far-off locations and sometimes even to other times in history. This is not lent much credence by critics, who insist on the precepts of locality and causality, but as our understanding of nature and technology becomes more quantum-like, one cannot help but feel that there may be some truth to such claims. However, proof, whether it is personal or consensual, is important, so I decided to attempt to have an OBE myself.

A Little Lesson in Chemistry

Since I discovered lucid dreaming, I have been able to become lucid in dreams with relative ease. The direct transition, however, was a challenge for me as I am not naturally inclined to meditation. For a direct transition, you allow your body to fall asleep, but you maintain a thread of mental awareness. This can take a couple of hours and is best performed in the middle of the night when one's brain chemistry is optimal. However, it can be difficult to silence one's mental chatter or indeed to stop oneself from falling asleep.

The reason it is so difficult to achieve a direct transition is that we are swimming upstream against the biological tides. Holding our attention normally requires the use of neurotransmitters. These are the chemicals that signal from one part of the brain to another part in order to give instructions. We need a sufficient quantity of neurotransmitters to activate the particular task. As an example, depression is caused in part by a lack of particular a particular neuro-chemical group known as the aminergic system. A drop in the production of these particular chemical agents leaves the person feeling isolated and unable to cope with life, whatever their personal circumstances.

This same chemical group dominates the brain when we are awake, keeping us alert, focused and in a good mood (most of the time). However, when we go to sleep the production of these messenger chemicals slows down. As this process begins, we see a reciprocal rise in the production of other chemicals, from the cholinergic group. The neurotransmitter is called acetylcholine and it is this agent that triggers REM sleep. So we have here a system resembling the ocean, with its ebbing and flowing tide. During our sleep cycles each night, there are progressively longer and more intense REM periods, with the final one lasting up to sixty minutes or more. This is because the cholinergic system is most active at this time and it is for this reason, lucid dreams are best attempted at this early stage of the morning (usually after four or five hours of sleep).

The difficulty faced by the potential lucid dreamer is that the brain will normally not allow the cholinergic system to fire up until the aminergic system has been depleted to a certain level. The point at which this occurs usually leaves the brain disoriented due to lack of the amines needed for focused awareness. One has to hold on to what little attention remains, while also trying to wrestle the choline-drenched dream. The problem is that the thread breaks easily, plunging the person into the dream and causing them to lose their lucidity. It takes a lot of practice before one meets with success.

The good news, however, is that we can facilitate the process by using a plant extract known as galantamine. Taken from the

Red Spider Lily plant, it was initially used as a food supplement to help boost the memory of patients who were at risk of developing Alzheimer's disease. The mechanism relies on the ability of the compound to tie up an enzyme known as acetylcholinesterase (ACE). When the brain functions normally, a special clean-up team mops away any excess neurotransmitters; in the case of acetylcholine, this falls to ACE. Galantamine acts on the ACE by tying up its receptors, effectively switching it off temporarily, preventing it from burning up the acetylcholine. This floods the cholinergic system, causing it to come on line prematurely in the sleep cycle. When taken appropriately, this can help improve memory by supplying the brain with the appropriate neurotransmitter needed to co-ordinate normal functioning.

Lucid dreaming is a by-product of this mechanism. The effects of galantamine on dreaming were initially reported by physicians as an incidental finding, but it was subsequently discovered by the lucid dreaming community and galamantine is now widely used to facilitate lucid dreaming. The strategy for someone attempting to have a direct transition lucid dream is to take galantamine after about 4-5 hours of sleep and then go back to bed. This forces the cholinergic system into action at a faster rate. We still need the aminergic system to drop to allow the cholinergic to change gears, but we have a brief window period during which the critical function remains active and REM sleep prematurely kicks in due to the bump in cholinergic activity. We can further stimulate the cholinergic system by using substitutes and stimulants like glycerophosphocholine (GPC) or nicotine. We then end up with the ideal neuro-chemical circumstances for a lucid dream – both the aminergic and the cholinergic systems activated simultaneously.

It is imperative to frame the use of galantamine appropriately. The agent helps change the brain chemistry to aid lucid dreaming, but unlike the psychedelic equivalent, it does not directly result in an altered state. Taking a large dose of galantamine will have no apparent effect on the waking mind. The agent is used to accentuate a particular biochemical event that occurs in the nocturnal phase of the body cycle and it really only has an impact then. When taken without attempting to lucid dream, it is possible that one will be triggered by the chemical shift alone, but it is unlikely. By the same token, if attempts to lucid dream with galantamine, it is not guaranteed to work, but it does help. Galantamine does give you vivid dreams though, which is what was initially reported by the patients taking it for memory treatment.

The legality of galantmaine is not currently a concern as it is considered a food supplement, which is more of a grey area. There has been a huge increase in the use of food supplements for body fitness in the last ten years and we are about to see a similar increase in the brain food industry. Galantmine fits into this group of foods, which are known as nootropics. In the case of lucid dreaming, we can substitute this with the term *oneirogen* to refer specifically to a dream enhancing nootropic.

'Advanced Lucid Dreaming - The Power of Supplements' is a fascinating text on the science of lucid dreaming. In his game-changing discussion of lucid dream supplements, Thomas Yuschak tells us about his experimental data involving galantamine as well as several other supplements. Yuschak is a chemical engineer taking a scientific look at how these agents affect lucid dreaming. The resulting essay is unsurpassed by any text on other this subject. Of particular interest is his finding that 90% of non-supplemented lucid dreams are of the indirect transition variety whereas 90% of the supplemented type takes the direct route. The reason for this is that the hybrid state of consciousness is prematurely forced into play, before the person loses consciousness to the act of sleeping.

We have now satisfied our dreaming model by showing that it is possible enter altered reality directly whilst maintaining composure and insight before returning to the ordinary state once more. This is underscored by both the biological theory as well as my own double-edge self-theory, which anticipates a yo-yoing of the critical function from fully functional to semi-functional and back again.

Although the biological mechanism is different than it would be with psychedelics, the principle is the same: a temporary dulling of the critical function. Experientially, too, both of these processes share some common ground, which I will now go on to discuss.

Psychedelics and Dreaming

With both the psychedelic and the direct transition lucid dream, we start from the waking critical state. We are in possession our cognitive functioning. In the physical dimension, causality and locality behave consistently. In both situations, as we drop into the altered state of reality, we experience a gradual loosening of the senses and sensibilities. The psychedelic and direct lucid transitions are usually heralded by a sense of withdrawal of attention and a feeling of going inside yourself. The eyes are usually closed in the case of the psychedelic (for a proper trip) and always in the case of the dream. A phenomenon known as hypnogogic hallucination tends to occur in both cases. This consists of internal visions parading in front of the subject's eyes. Typically these visions consist of geometric shapes and wallpaper-like patterns, with bright colours and flowing sequences.

In the case of the dream, one has aural hallucinations too; these consist of buzzing, hissing and vibrating noises in the head. Although this can be a feature of the psychedelic trip too, it is less common. Bodily sensations occur in both situations, but they are experienced differently. The psychedelic makes the body feel heavy and tired whereas the dream usually makes the body feel light and weightless. However, this is not a rule and one can experience all kinds of sensations in both states. The lightness of the body can result in a feeling that one is floating, which can trigger an out-of-body experience. The psychedelic may also have some peripheral body sensations, such as nausea and/or vomiting, but this is never a feature of the dream.

Disorientation and a sense of detachment are common to both transitions. One can feel as though they are unable to hang onto the ordinary world as they fall into a more unfamiliar state. This can cause one to prematurely abort the transition in the case of the dream but this is not possible for the psychedelic pilgrim. This is due to a disintegration of the ego, which is being diluted by the swelling of the chemistry. Panic can set in as the ego drowns and the person can feel as though death is eminent. It is best not to resist this experience, but this is easier said than done, so one should be prepared before undertaking such a journey.

The process gradually escalates and the hallucinations become more frequent and congruent, ultimately forging more complex things like objects, faces and landscapes (any vision is possible). A loose narrative starts to bind the scenes together as parts of the scenery start to interact with each other. This is usually followed by a sense that we can actually start to participate. In the case of the psychedelic, the mind alone is used to navigate the experience. In the case of the dream, however, the dream body becomes part of the hallucination, allowing one to enter the scene and navigate it in a familiar, corporeal way. This is one big difference between the two situations: the psychedelicist's body remains rooted in ordinary reality whereas the dreamer is completely immersed.

Although it is possible to experience a full shift in the state of reality with a sufficiently high dose of a psychedelic mixture, this does not usually occur. This means we can still experience the ordinary state of our world to an extent, although it may appear grossly distorted and terrifically disorienting (depending on the dose). One can fully transition into the magic state on psychedelics, but this is a lot less common and should be attempted with caution. The lucid dream, on the other hand, insists on the full transition; there is a complete shift from critical ordinary reality to the semi-critical quantum state.

I am not sure where I stand on this matter of having a partial versus a full transition. The latter is signified by the complete transformation of one's environment, including one's body. One might wonder whether the degree to which the critical function is shifted away from its baseline ordinary state towards the pre-critical, quantum state would act to define the physics of our world and whether we fully or partially transition. On this basis, I speculate that the dream body can step on stage only when the ego is sufficiently diminished to allow an alternative sense of self to emerge. On this note, my model suggests that the ability to shape-shift into animals and various other beings, as well as inanimate objects, something both lucid dreamers and psychedelic practitioners report alike, is facilitated by a sufficiently tamed critical function. I suspect they are able to change their perceptual form by diffusing the ego construct while still maintaining some degree of narrative awareness. I have done this to varying degrees myself and I suspect that highly trained shamanic people like the Native Americans would be able to achieve incredible expressions of themselves as various forms and beings.

In many tribal traditions shape-shifting into animal forms helps the hunter gather information about the game he or she is pursuing, offering him or her insight into when and where to hunt in order to bring food to the tribe. This brings us back to the question of non-local consciousness. Is it possible to be somewhere other than where our bodies are in the ordinary world or is what we perceive in these altered states exclusive to our own minds? The answer to this question requires us to consider our model in more detail. In order to do this, we will need to home in on our ever elusive Factor X.

The Paradox of Lucid Dreaming

9) Monkeys, Mushrooms and UFOs

In my quest for understanding, I have had two agendas to satisfy: that of my explorer self and that of my scientific self. The former leans towards personal experience while the latter requires validation from fellow observers. In order to construct a credible theory of reality I consider the consensual view the necessary prerogative here. However any stance I take will only ever resonate with a select proportion of people as there will always be limitations to how well I can describe the world to others and vice versa. This results in an intellectual hiatus, which is further fortified by cultural institutions that have been built up in people's minds.

Take the example of a UFO arriving on our planet. In the Western world, we have the term 'unidentified flying object' to contend with as it causes us to immediately consign the UFO to the realm of ignorance. A culture that already had forged a psycho-social template for the idea of aliens would see this as a prophecy as the culture would already have a frame to accommodate it. It would not be seen as a breach in reality, not in the way it might in our society.

In our case, the cultural resistance to this event would be so rigid that the experience itself could even become unperceivable to us. This sounds tautological as we cannot be aware of that which we do not perceive, so how could we prove there aren't already things in our presence of which we are not ordinarily aware? We might look to the famous story of the Native Americans who, it is claimed, could not see Columbus' ships when his crew hit land. It is alleged that although the ships on the shore were visible to the people, those further out at sea were invisible to them as their perceptual barriers were too strong to permit the ships to become part of their reality. The idea that ships could sail so far from land was inconceivable to them. It was not until the shaman saw the ships and shouted this to his tribe that their perceptual barriers were raised. As the visionary of the group, their trust in his sight allowed them to see the ships too. Whether or not this story is true, it fits well with our theory so far so let's revise that a little now.

Earlier in the book, we questioned the nature of reality and how we might define it. Our discussion took us into the world of dreams, where we noted the similarities between waking and dreaming. We also brought on stage the lucid dreamer, with his or her unique ability to explore both states of consciousness. We saw that there are many types of lucid dreamers, from the scientific Western-minded type to the Eastern Buddhist, as well as the South American shaman and the pigmy witchdoctor of the African jungle. Each group has their own view of reality and although there is some ontological agreement among the various peoples, there is also a great degree of variation in their respective philosophies too.

The Western frame employs physics as its modus operandi. This is a monophasic perspective as it holds that there is only one fundamental reality and that everything else is an expression of it. When reality is altered for the individual, this is considered a pseudo-reality and is thought of as relatively trivial. This view of reality is successful because it is testable on certain philosophical levels but it is finally starting to give way due to our understanding of quantum mechanics.

When we looked inside the atom, the great discovery that awaited us was not just that it consisted mostly of empty space, but that what matter there was proved to be very elusive. Matter is not something we can easily describe as it has an unusual quality that causes us problems: uncertainty. Matter, under experimental evaluation, is revealed to have pairs of properties that have a complementary relationship, which means that when we describe one, we affect the other in a mostly unpredictable way. Examples include position and velocity, as well as time and energy. This is not due to our measuring technology, as some misinterpret, but actually points to a deeper truth at the heart of nature, in the mathematical equations upon which our world is built.

Not only does the action of the observer upset the behaviour of matter, there is also evidence that there is no matter to speak of at all, until a conscious being interacts with it. This is just like a dream as we expect the dreamer to influence the dream world and only expect things to be present in a dream when they are witnessed by the dreamer.

We then took our discussion into the world of neurobiology and looked for trends in the data available about altered states. We discovered that the ability to influence the architecture of one's reality adequately was limited by the presence or absence of a critical self-reflective mind-set. This could be shifted up and down on a scale. The critical function, as we termed it, was found to oscillate naturally over the course of the day. As a result, we slip into a less congruent state of reality for brief periods each day. This is called dreaming. It is not exclusive to humans and we suspect it has advantages for both the organism and the planet as a whole, although we have not yet identified these. Furthermore, this state of consciousness may have adverse effects, as is the case with some psychiatric conditions.

The shifting of consciousness into different states is controlled by body chemistry. In a healthy person this does not present any problems, even though we enter into a temporary state of insanity every night. In a non-consensual experience of reality, such as schizophrenia, we have seen how Western society treats this as a medical condition whereas the indigenous peoples of the planet see it as a gift. In their world, the 'madman' becomes the medium or adviser and the healer. This highlights the influence of culture on our view of reality.

Although we are not usually critically aware in altered states it is possible to enter them with varying degrees of critical focus by using a plethora of techniques. These include dreaming, dancing, drumming, singing, consuming certain plants, as well as meditation. Methods of inducing altered states are becoming a common subject of discussion online as more and more people are questioning the validity of their reality. The information outflow from the internet is dissolving cultural barriers to perception. This might be gradually disarming our critical mind-sets by offering us new and radically different narrative constructs of reality. I propose that reality itself is changing due to the cross-cultural fertilisation facilitated by the exponential growth of information technology.

The double-edge self-theory proposes that what toggles reality from an ordinary to an altered state is the critical function and that the relationship is reciprocal, i.e. the more critically self-aware we become, the more rigidly reality behaves. If we adopt the pre-critical view – reality softens, as in dreaming, whereas a more classically coherent reality is consistent with a critical mind. The biology that precipitates the critical function can be pushed in either direction as desired. I propose that something like my push-ups test would correlate to a simultaneous increase or decrease in the brain organelles that configure self-reflective awareness. Known collectively as the default mode network (DFM), we are already seeing promising evidence here of the ability to change the nature of perception by stimulating or dulling the system. We considered, by implication, that perhaps the notion of an objective physical reality might be an inadequate description of how things are and instead we considered a spectrum of activity, determined by the coherence of the observer. We speculated that the world might act in an orderly fashion at one end of the scale, as in ordinary consciousness and classical physics, and that it would appear to be far more flexible at the other end, exhibiting properties like non-locality, retro-causality and probability. This quantum end of the scale would be consistent with the pre-critical (dreaming) or semi-critical (lucid dreaming and psychedelics) mind-set.

Of particular merit here are the recent laboratory studies on lucid dreaming and psychedelic drugs. These altered states of consciousness offer us great insight when viewed with brain scanning equipment. Although each pushes the critical function from opposite ends of the spectrum, they both have the same effect: they shift it towards the centre of the scale, where a hybrid reality emerges. The quantum weirdness of dreaming mixes with the more sedate physics of the ordinary world. But the question remains whether it is possible to bend space and time or whether this is merely a product of our own perception?

The answer, I suspect, will be found in the consensual experience of altered reality but this is proving challenging to achieve. The double-edge self-theory, however, does predict it and so I am looking for Factor X, the missing link between the two states of ordinary and quantum reality which might bridge them for a number of individual observers.

I will now reveal Factor X and discuss how I think we might utilise it to build a more flexible future. I will begin by directing your attention to the first magicians that walked the planet – I am, of course, speaking about our ancestor, the shaman ...

Return of the Shaman

There are two reasons why I am starting with the shaman. The first is that he/she is the master of plant medicine. Psychedelics, as I have already outlined, allow us the luxury of starting from the point of view of the ordinary critical-consensual world. Approaching the matter from this end we can navigate towards the hybrid state without losing consciousness. This is not always the case with dreaming, which usually necessitates sleeping (unless we employ the more rare direct transition). The second reason why I am beginning with the shaman is because his/her practice is the earliest known form of altered reality, which could have far-reaching implications in determining how our state of consciousness came into being in the first place.

Our shamanologist friend, Terrence McKenna, came up with what I would say is one of the most shocking theories in human history. It involves monkeys and magic mushrooms on the plains of Africa and proposes how those monkeys might have evolved into you and me. The *stoned ape theory*, as it is called, suggests that modern humans first appeared on the evolutionary stage somewhere in the last couple of hundred thousand years. According to McKenna, our ability to perform abstract reasoning is what makes us unique. This gives us the ability to reflect, learn and plan. McKenna suggests that we are the top predator in terms of intellect because of our unique way of processing information.

He speculates that a chance encounter between our African ancestors, the great ape, and psilocybin-containing mushrooms, many years ago, might have caused our brains to double in capacity within an unprecedented period of time. I feel that McKenna has nailed it and the only reason we have not heard more about this theory is because it has been smothered by the same conservative thinking that Darwin faced in his day. I believe McKenna's theory will grow more popular as we uncover some of the deeper secrets of the psychedelic experience. Nothing affects the human imagination more profoundly than the psychedelic compound. But the question remains: what exactly does it do and how does this fit with McKenna's theory?

McKenna says that the answer is in the biology. He describes a curious state of consciousness called synaesthesia, whereby one's sensory inputs can cross-contaminate each other so one can smell colours, see sounds or hear tastes. Synaesthesia is also found outside of the psychedelic experience and there are people who experience their reality this way on a daily basis. Mozart is said to have been able to see sound as colour patterns.

One can experience this classic synaesthetic phenomenon oneself on about 2g of dried magic mushrooms (or 20g of fresh produce). A couple of hours after consumption, when the chemistry peaks, one can introduce some rock music, close one's eyes and watch the imagery respond to it. If the style of music is changed, the imagery will change dramatically. It's fascinating if one wants to explore this theory on a more personal level.

The shaman has been experiencing this for countless centuries and has learned to use the experience to develop his/her ability to hold the space during psychedelic ceremony. The shaman almost always plays music when using the plant. This guides the vision of the group by fashioning the imagery around certain themes, thus indirectly preventing other images from entering the collective mind. Theoretically it could even be possible for him/her to invoke specific images with special songs known as *icaros* by the people of the Amazon. Many people do report such events during psychedelic ceremonies, especially with a native brew known as ayahuasca.

Ayahuasca is a drink, native to the Amazonian Americans, which contains dimethyltryptamine (DMT) in a digestible form. It is taken mostly during a group ceremony for healing purposes. The shaman directs the energy of the group with his/her enchanting music and dance, which is intended to prevent other energy forms or spirits from entering the space. One can only speculate about the validity of such matters for so long until intellectual curiosity drives one to experience it for oneself. McKenna's brother Dennis, another light in the world of shamanism today, refers to this as the ultimate sceptic test. We know very little of the real power of the plant, in the Western world but I believe that the shaman who has spent many generations working with the plant does possess this knowledge and that we should follow the shaman away from the degradation of nature towards a higher dimension of being.

In constructing a model of consensual altered reality, as is proposed by our last cardinal difference between waking and dreaming, the shaman with his/her music serves as an excellent example. We have a group of people witnessing a similar event, which is unperceivable to non-participating bystanders. To the non-psychedelic witness there would be no visions to speak of and yet the plant-consuming group might all agree on what they saw. Although this is the not exact evidence needed to qualify the out of body experience as a possible non-local event, it does lend some credence to the polyphasic view which would be required to accommodate it. The hull of conventional scientific thinking is not being breached by the group hallucination here and yet it would surely feel eerie to the Western mind to consider that such a reality could co-exist with our own in such a casual manner. This does not satisfy the particulars of the OBE but it I'm sure I harmonise with McKenna when I suggest that we are due an upgrade to our cultural operating system, one which will allow for orthogonal states of consciousness to interact with each other, as is suggested by the speculated out of body condition.

Cows and Consciousness

McKenna's real breakthrough comes when he proposes how the psychedelic agent may have helped to forge the language we speak today. He asserts that the psychedelic compound causes the language centre of the brain to erupt into hyper-glossolalia, i.e. speaking in tongues. Curiously, this condition is synonymous with both the insane and religious ecstasy. The idea that language is close to the crazy or the divine is noted by McKenna, who points our attention to the quotation from the Bible, 'In the beginning was the word'. His theory is far too immersive to explain in detail here, but I can say is that it is a very convincing one. The basic thrust of the argument is that our ancestral primates were forced out of the trees due to ecological change and had to forage the land for new dietary avenues. It was here, he proposes, that they would have first encountered the mushrooms, probably in the dung of cows. The consumption of the fungus would have triggered, among other things, a form of synaesthesia, giving the animals the ability to encourage images to form in each other's minds by making small mouth noises and matching physical signals. Outlandish though this may seem, consider it for a moment. If I verbally ask you to think of an 'elephant dressed in a tutu', it appears your mind. What you are experiencing with this complex form of precise sound and imagery may have its roots in a far more rudimentary grunting and signing which would eventually become words and symbols in the mind.

One cannot help but speculate how religion and ceremony might have emerged from these mystical states as the monkeys filled their bellies with mushrooms and their minds with images of terrific shapes and colours, which would otherwise have been completely unfamiliar to them. It may be no coincidence that cows became sacred animals as they were pursued in search of the gold that grew from their dung. This may indeed be the heritage of the Hindus, who still continue worship cows to this day. Needless to say, this is not how the holy man of India will see it, as the actual narrative would have been long whitewashed by various myths and ceremonies to accommodate this often amusing celebration of the bovine deity.

Scientific support is gradually growing this view and there is significant anthropological evidence. It is becoming widely accepted that the first signs of self-reflective awareness might be on the walls of our oldest caves. Ancient paintings of people and animals, as well as geometric grammar, the likes of which we see in the hynogogic state of consciousness, can be dated to about thirty five thousand years ago, which fits McKenna's theory. His theory allows for a quick transition from simple primates to self-reflective hominids as language allows each generation to inform the next, causing an exponential increase in complexity over the course of time. This amounts to is a rapid shift in the ability of our ape ancestors to communicate with each other and thus compete and succeed in their respective environments.

Nature favours complexity. This explosion in opportunity is mirrored by the advancement of computer technology today. Moore's Law states that 'over the history of computing hardware, the number of transistors in a dense integrated circuit doubles approximately every two years'. Broadly speaking, this means that communication technology moves at a frantic rate and produces massive changes in the world in increasingly short bursts over a given time period. This echoes my description of what is currently happening to our reality, thanks to the symbiosis of the mobile phone and the internet. I believe we are currently experiencing a wave of conscious evolution, which will eventually prove to be as significant as that of the eruption of language eighty or a hundred thousand years ago.

McKenna also proposes that the paintings on cave walls of people engaged in activities, such as hunting, suggests that they had achieved significant intellectual insight, unlocking a higher dimension of consciousness. He suggests that it is this third–person relationship to the world that defines self-reflective thinking in the human and thus the paintings of our ancestors, by implication, are the first expression of us as higher mammals. This is a powerful idea. My own conclusion is that it does indeed hold water. I cemented my own view on the matter a couple of years ago when I attended a 'Gateways of the Mind' conference in London. The final piece of the puzzle fell into place when an audience member posed a question to the panel of experts at the event: 'Do animals have lucid dreams?'

This question needs to be answered in two parts. Firstly we need to consider whether or not animals dream at all and secondly we need to consider the matter of lucidity and how we might go about proving whether or not animals are capable of lucid dreams. Our observation of brain activity in animals indicates REM sleep and, more generally, their sleeping patterns are consistent with our own. The fact that their biology and behaviour resembles our own so closely has prompted many to conclude that they dream but of course we cannot be certain what that would constitute in the mind of the animal. That animals do dream tells us something important about our world: dreaming must have a very specific biological function. My intellectual compass points once more to the critical function and its cyclical oscillation.

I envision a brief period in each animal's reality during which the critical function is pushed aside to allow a pre-critical quantum state to emerge. This, according to my model, stimulates the animal to interact with its reality in a more flexible manner. I believe this allows new behaviour patterns to be tried and tested without fear of harm or failure. The animal, I expect, is then more capable of adopting new behaviour strategies when forced to do so by inevitable environmental changes, meaning that it has a better chance of survival and, as such, is more likely to pass on their genes. For this reason, I think that all higher animals dream; it is because they dream that they can adapt to and overcome environmental challenges. Likewise, it is because we can dream beyond our circumstances that we can come up with new ideas, which eventually become our reality. Dreaming therefore acts as a catalyst for complexity and nature always favours more complexity because it encourages more stability in the ecological system.

With this in mind, we can see that animals must dream because behaviour is inherently plastic and therefore needs to be bent into shape. However I believe the more complex question of lucidity can only be considered by introducing language into the equation. I believe that one needs to have sufficiently abstract language skills in order to have a lucid dream as the realisation that one is lucid in a dream necessitates the intellectual idea of dreaming as something that happens in our minds when we are asleep. This is a complex notion, which remains unresolved even in our own understanding. For an animal to have the cognitive insight necessary to forge a word like 'dream' in their vocabulary seems highly unlikely. Thus I expect that animals dream in the pre-critical manner only.

The moment we realise we are dreaming, the sensory modalities remain unperturbed, which is to say that they do not necessarily change. We still hear with our ears, see through our eyes and touch with our fingers, albeit those of our dream bodies. Thus the change in perception is taking place on the intellectual rather than the sensual level. This is a domain of experience normally restricted to higher life forms and the quality of activity in this arena is ordained by the complexity of an organism's internal syntax. It is for this reason that I propose that lucid dreaming is an ability that is sanctioned by the evolution of a sufficiently sophisticated language centre and hence something we only see in advanced cerebro-social systems.

And so *language is our Factor X.* It is because we have self-reflective language that we can discriminate between our various states of consciousness. It is through language that we have left the familiar ground of classic physics and entered the quantum world. And it is because we think the way that we do that we can even talk about it in the first place, both to each other and, more importantly, to ourselves.

It is this inner voice that asks the crucial question, 'Am I dreaming?' Only you can answer that question, which is possible only with recourse to language. I believe language completes our theory as it allows us to build an arbitrary construct of reality through which we can enter the hybrid semi-critical state of consciousness.

McKenna's Model

The inner voice is the key to our consciousness. We are contemplative creatures, which means that we think about our circumstances a lot. To be human is to introspect; it is to apply meaning to our world with abstract concepts like art, humour and poetry. Therefore it is perhaps no coincidence that magic mushrooms make one laugh hysterically for no rational reason and that, on another level, they can show you visions of such profundity that you feel compelled to express them in an artistic fashion.

One can picture the first shaman shivering in pain and ecstasy, perched in the corner of some ancient cave, his mind full of mystery, his mouth full of mushrooms, and his finger ready to transmit what he learnt in his heightened state of consciousness. This image heralds the beginning of a revolution in the way nature experiences itself as it is through us that the cosmos hears and feels; it is through our eyes that it sees and knows, and it is through our actions that it ultimately expresses itself. And so it was not just man that uttered his first words all those years ago; it was, in fact, the universe itself. We are the inheritors of this same dialogue today, but now it has complexified into a myriad of intellectual vectors, each one catalysing the whole system.

McKenna harmonises this motif with his own 'novelty theory'. This is his speculation that time itself may be speeding up and that this will inevitably result in a climax of some kind. It is impossible to anticipate what this might look like, but I believe it is already happening, as did McKenna. He anticipated that he might see the concrescence in his own lifetime and perhaps he didn't as he died at the young age of 53, but I feel that the signs of his vision are apparent and that the final ingredient we needed to make it happen is now in the mix.

Novelty theory is all about complexity. McKenna proposes that there are two opposing forces at work in the universe: conservative repetition, or what he calls habit, and its opposite, novelty. Novelty is the creative and progressive front whereby habit acts to stabilise the system. The two are in a cosmic tug of war but novelty, according to McKenna, has the edge and it is novelty that is propelling the cosmos into increasingly more elaborate expressions, which sits well with my own theory about why we dream (to increase complexity in the organic system).

McKenna looked at time as a measurement of novel data in a system. He suggested that the universe was showing mathematical patterns in its history that alluded to intervals of hyper-novel information in the system. Each one is more or less equivalent in impact to the last but they occur with increasing frequency. He wrote a computer programme called Time Wave Zero to examine this. The programme maps out the information process as being either novel or habitual and we discover a repetitive arrangement of oscillating wave-type action. The peaks on this graph of waves represent novelty whereas the troughs indicate habit.

He then introduces the idea of the fractal, a mathematical concept which, in the case of the time wave, basically states that any small part of the wave will have the same fundamental characteristics as a larger fraction of the wave. This kind of patterning causes a self-replicating process to occur within the system. McKenna proposes that this is why each generation needed less time to attain a similar transaction of information as the last, suggesting that the cosmos itself was becoming exponentially complex by consequence.

He begins mapping out the discourse of activity at time zero, the Big Bang. He describes the universe as a very simple place with only the most basic of chemistry to contend with. For the first five or so billion years, nothing much occurs. If we consider the universe as being approximately 13.7 billion years old, that means there was a long time during which it was a quiet place with little change or novelty being expressed over large spans of time. But when life first appears, a plethora of possibilities come into play and it is from then on that we see a sharp transition in the time wave, just as one would anticipate activity to occur in an exponential system.

McKenna goes on to give examples of when there were peaks in the novelty system, such as the birth of our self-reflective awareness and the dropping of the atomic bomb but I think a criticism needs to be made here; the system suffers from a major flaw in that the specifics of the particular events, like those mentioned above, are almost impossible to pinpoint and/or quantify. Language, as an example, can be argued to be pivotal in our development and would certainly imply something of an exponential design, but it would prove almost impossible to build any real kind of statistical argument to express this as it's beyond mathematical calculation due to the virtually infinite number of potential variables involved.

Likewise one might think the choice of events poses problems. Was it the bombing of Hiroshima or that of Pearl Harbour that we should look at as the swell of the wave? Perhaps it is the making of the bomb or even the splitting of the atom. We might even point to Einstein's famous equation, which paved the way for this, or perhaps his birth? The point is that we can regress the model to wherever we like and hence retro-fit it to accommodate our model, which really isn't sound scientific structure.

However, if we take a top-level view of this theory and agree that what it implies is an exponential algorithm of sorts, we can agree that there is a sense of this happening today, perhaps especially in the last ten years. I have even heard people say that they feel time is moving more quickly. I have felt this way too. We say that time goes fast when we are having fun and perhaps having fun means experiencing something novel. If we follow McKenna's line of thinking on this, the system will eventually reach a cosmic conclusion, which he refers to as 'the transcendental object at the end of time'. This is such a powerful idea that it seems unfair to reduce it to words so I will only briefly allude to what it implies. He envisioned an end to time and space. He predicted that history itself would conclude when the system had finally run its course and the final climactic shift had occurred.

According to his calculations the 'escathon' would occur in 2012, which was consistent with the predictions of Mayan shamans thousands of years ago. Incidentally, McKenna claimed he was unaware of their prediction when he was coming up with his own, although there is some dispute about whether or not this is true. At the risk of sounding like a doomsday cult devotee, I think it is important to allow for a little flexibility when we consider his prediction post-2012. Most of us probably do not feel such an event has occurred but I suggest we take a moment to consider things here before we cast our final judgment. Metaphorically speaking, we know from biology that the body can carry a disease long before it shows any symptoms. Perhaps in a similar manner, our consciousness might carry truths which remain unknown to us as of yet.

I believe that McKenna's prediction was late and not premature, as many might suggest, for it is my view that he flagged the birth of the internet. I believe we are now hopelessly entangled in the internet, being pulled towards each other, enhancing our ability to interact in increasingly complex ways.

We are experiencing a digital revolution and both you and I are central to the process because it is our views and actions that are making a difference. The world no longer belongs to the elite. It is a work in progress. As we leave behind the old plague of oppressive ideas that only served those who sold them, it is time to rejoice and relish the promise of pure possibility. In today's world anyone can have a voice and most people worldwide can find out just about anything. Truth no longer has any real meaning as it is up to us to decide what we want to hear and who we want to hear it from. This is not some kind of anarchic dystopia that I am describing, but a different kind of story which sets the tone for a more meaningful future, a future in which we might live in peace and harmony through mutual agreement and higher understanding of what the word 'truth' actually means. But this battle has been fought for many years and countless lives have been lost to it for it is a war that has been fought not on the battlefields of our kingdoms but in our own minds, for it is here that the ultimate prize is to be won. 'Imagination' is a word that is becoming increasingly familiar to our ears. This is a sign of the times; we are finally waking up to the idea that, in many ways, this is what our world is actually made of.

My Take on the Theory

The universe today is expanding exponentially which is to say that it is increasing in size at a faster rate at every moment. This lends itself to what physicists refer to as entropy or chaos. Entropy means that the degree of disorder in the system is increasing. Western scientists see this as the universe falling apart and eventually becoming a pointless, meaningless mess. But I suggest that, in much the same way the critical function slips out the way for the sentient mind in order to interrupt repetitive behaviour habits and encourage more novel strategies to emerge, entropy too encourages more complexity in the cosmic system. It does so by constantly breaking it down and challenging it to be re-built in more novel and intricate ways. My vision is of an outward flow of random activity that is widely diffused over time until it reaches a drag force, which condenses it and forces an immediate increase in complexity. This, I suggest, is facilitated by the emergence of self-reflective language, which allows the universe itself to introspect through our thoughts and introduce change through our actions. My theory is that abstract language has trapped the outward chaotic flow of information and forged an intergalactic feedback mechanism which compresses activity into a higher frequency dynamic, thus changing the gear of the whole operation.

It is because of our understanding of our place in the cosmos that we, the introspective atomic enterprise, can look to the future and expect to prevail where the dinosaurs once perished. We may succeed in avoiding the same catastrophic end because we have one tool they did not have: self-reflective language, the ability to share ideas with each other and use our conclusions to develop elaborate defence mechanisms. We may even shoot an asteroid down one day, the likes of which wiped out our predecessors on this planet once upon a time. It seems to me that we are heading towards an inevitable change in our consciousness and right at the centre of this stage is a cocktail of language, information technology, lucid dreaming and psychedelics.

Psychedelics have much to teach us about our world and they do so in a most peculiar way. 'Ayahuasca' (the plant brew I mentioned earlier) is a very special word because it has three different meanings. The first is the name of the vegetation itself. The second meaning of the word describes it as a healing medicine used by some indigenous societies both historically and today. It is taken either directly by the patient or, in some cases, by the shaman, who then heals the patient from his/her altered state. This notion of the doctor taking the medicine in order to heal the patient would seem absurd to a Western mind but it fits into the shaman's world. This is underlined by the third meaning the word. It can be used to refer to the spirit that allegedly occupies the plant. This being, often considered a female entity, is the one who offers teaching and healing. The shaman acts as the conduit for the spirit and cures the patient from this perspective. This is a difficult paradigm for the Western mind to accommodate. It is easy to dismiss the idea until one consumes the plant.

If one is brave enough to ingest the plant mixture, one can enter into what can only be described as a mental dialogue between yourself and what seems to be another being in your mind. Most psychedelic plants cause an internal dialogue between you and another seemingly sentient agency in the head. In many cases the inner voice acts as a teacher that wants to show you how to improve your life. The teacher-student relationship is not always the same – sometimes it's friendly, sometimes it's harsh, but there is usually an implied hierarchy between you and the plant as it teaches you a deeper understanding of the world.

Regardless of the semantics of the relationship, what is pertinent here is the sense that one is experiencing multidimensional thinking, i.e. interacting with two parts of the mind in different ways. Whether we consider the other voice to be an independent consciousness or a fragment of our own, the fact remains that one must consider this dichotomous mind instrumental in laying the tracks for our own self-reflective thinking. This in turn would have forged the backbone of our critical function, as well as the space-time mechanics of causality. It is my view, therefore, that the encounter between the monkey and the mushroom resulted in what we call reality today. It is this reality that is now going into overdrive due to our ability to comment on our state of consciousness to anyone, anywhere, with our hyper-technical microchips and quantum-produced transistor processors.

If it was our chance meeting with the plant that catalysed our consciousness, allowing it to divide and interact with itself, then we must ask what this same plant could do for us today, if only we put it to good use. I have already commented on how the critical function can be temporarily dismantled to allow for a more dream-like state of mind to dominate and how this, in turn, encourages more complex behaviour to emerge in the species.

What separates us from the rest of nature is our unique form of language. As we untie ourselves from the chains of our primate bodies, it is not only our big brains but also our wondrous words that we will carry with us, for it is our self-reflective lexicon, the very essence of what makes a lucid dream possible, that makes us the greatest explorers that the universe has ever known.

The Paradox of Lucid Dreaming

10) The End is the Beginning is the End

As our trip together reaches its conclusion, we can reflect on dreaming and what it could mean in light of what we have discussed. It is because we are able to enter into a dialogue with each other as well as ourselves that the world holds its shape. Without the critical language frame, we would experience chaos, a disjointed and non-causal world. The thing that binds our world together is language; it is because we can string a narrative together that our circumstances have any roots in reality at all. The non-lucid dreaming mind does not exhibit this complex internal dialogue and it is for this reason that it does not exhibit a strictly causal mechanism.

Nothing could be more telling than the contrast between ordinary and lucid dreaming. We observed that it is the self-reflective lexicon that allows us to shift into the lucid mode. 'Am I dreaming?' we ask. This enquiry into the nature of our state is sophisticated and requires us to have already invested in a specific kind of cultural operating system so as to differentiate between waking and dreaming, identifying them as two different states of reality. For this we need an equally sophisticated syntax.

The phase transition in consciousness that we are currently experiencing is happening on many levels but I believe language is the key because our current problem with physics does not arise from our experimental apparatus design but from our inability to articulate our findings in a manner which makes sense. We are forced to look at matters from a number of different perspectives, which stand in stark contrast to each other but are said to act in a complementary fashion. This means that we can only speak about the qualities as a co-ownership of the event. The conventional view physics tends to be black and white, but all we can find, as we dig deeper into the subatomic world, are many shades of grey.

Grey might even be a misleading term as matters seem to be far more elusive than conclusive on the subatomic level. Nature behaves unpredictably and even paradoxically. A paradox, we said, is a statement that apparently contradicts itself and at the same time may be true. The operative word here is 'apparently' as it alludes to the possibility that the contradiction is a product of the observer's perspective.

We must appreciate the importance of language here, as we consider the possibility that the conscious observer might have more of an influence on the formation of reality than we had previously thought. The conclusions of quantum physics are undeniable; we are somehow influencing our own reality by the manner in which we investigate it. McKenna would say that, 'The world is made of language'; he was indicating the way in which we described reality, that it could only ever be a function of our own examination. We can see how the critical language frame gives us a narrative script that allows us to hold time, space and causality all together. I would even speculate that the model of physics we are so familiar with today would fall apart without it. No doubt there would be a world out there without language to perceive it, but it would surely behave in a very different way. I am proposing that physics itself is a function of language and that the way in which we experience our world, whether we are awake, dreaming or something in between, is orchestrated by our ability to articulate it (or not, as the case may sometimes be).

The reality that we are all familiar with is fashioned by the theory of classical physics, which has proved valuable to us as it has helped explain how things work and has given birth to countless technological innovations. However, as we head off into the future this perspective is starting to feel heavy. I think the reason for this is that our intuitive view of the world, which is supported by the classical physical model, does not fit with the experimental data on the quantum level. So I want to propose that the paradox we are experiencing is not an irresolvable fact but actually a perceptual hiatus that can be bridged by adopting a more advanced language frame.

The current common perceptual view our world is 'dualistic'. By this I mean that we construct our world from the point of view of a subject witnessing an object. So we get an 'I', which is observing, and the 'that', which is being observed. This approach implies that the two are inherently independent and that either can exist without the other, but does this add up? Our intuition says it does – after all, we sense that there is a world out there, which was here before we were born and will remain after we die. Physics has always championed this sense of an objective world and it has arguably been able to justify its position. One could suggest, as scientists often do, that the technological success of classical physics is a testament to its ontological triumph but, in truth, the cracks in this model have been showing for some time and, paradoxically, they were flagged by one of its greatest proponents.

In his famous equation, $E=MC2$, Einstein showed that time, the thing that ties our world together, was not entirely objective. Time was discovered to be dependent on the speed of the observer. According to Einstein, the faster we move towards the speed of light, the slower time becomes and at the speed of light itself (if it were possible to reach it), there would be no sense of time at all. This should have sent shockwaves through the physics community and in many ways it did, but it was also brushed aside because the effects are only noticeable at extremely high velocities, so it is not something that affects us in our ordinary everyday life. But I feel we are finally being forced to reconsider our position. It is the impact of cross–culturalisation, being driven by the information revolution, which is now pushing us to address the obvious faults in our epistemological perspective.

If we adopt a literal view of the world we have to describe situations as either this way or that way, but never both ways at the same time. This sounds sensible until we try to isolate any of these qualities. Imagine left coming onto the stage of the cosmos and right only showing up ten minutes later. This does not make any sense at all. Left and right are like day and night or black and white; they imply each other and one cannot exist without the other. Bohr defined these qualities as complementary pairs.

Complementary pairs are not limited to the quantum scale. They are everywhere in our world – up and down, smile and frown, etc. Niels Bohr was acutely aware of what the quantum revolution had unearthed. He recognised the true meaning of the uncertainty principle; he could see that matter was inherently undefinable as this or that and could only be considered as a hybrid of the two. This pointed the finger at the relationship between the observer and the object; could either be defined without considering the other? The answer is no, in the same way one cannot consider a dream without recognising the role of the dreamer.

Take as an example the bee and its ability to see the infrared scale of light. We mentioned previously that the bee would see a flower very differently to how we see it. The flower is thus only ever a measure of the observation technology which is interacting with it. Our apparatus, as humans, is an optical nerve, fixed to our modern cerebral cortex. This gives us a very different picture of the flower. A cat, by contrast, will not see what either we or the bee will see as cats are technically colour-blind. They lack the red cone cells we possess to give us the spectrum of colours we can see. So what colour is a flower really? The truth is that it depends on who is observing it.

The argument that there is a reality out there, which can reduced objectively, regardless of who is witnessing it, has hit too many hurdles to be taken seriously anymore. If we are really paying attention to the lessons of nature, we should take heed of the notion that nothing is truly separate, that we are as connected now as we were when all matter in the universe was compressed to the size of a pea, some 13.7 billion or so years ago. The only thing that has changed is our perception of the process. Our priority now should be to recognise this possibility in order to build new schemas that can accommodate it and to evolve our language.

Shifting the Language Frame

Niels Bohr was certain too that language was where we should look. He remarked that, 'We are trapped by language to such a degree that every attempt to formulate insight is a play on words.' He was referring to the tautological paradox presented to us by language: that any discussion of it would be limited by the very thing that was being used to examine it. He asserted that syntax was somehow written into the fabric of physics and by examining other communication systems we might come to a deeper understanding of nature. He did, in his own lifetime, indicate how we might begin to fashion such an idiom.

On being awarded a prestigious prize in Denmark, known as the Order of the Elephant, he was asked to present a coat of arms for display on the Wall of Fame at Frederiksborg Castle. As Bohr was one of only two scientists ever given the honour, normally reserved for royalty or distinguished generals, he did not already have a coat of arms and so decided to design one himself. The logo he chose to represent his philosophy was the Tai-Chi symbol of Chinese Taoist origin. This is the familiar symbol seen below. Tai-Chi means 'Great Polarity' and it alludes to the inherent change that drives the engine of the cosmos.

The Taoists, in Bohr's view, had forged a deep relationship with semiotics. They recognised that no two moments in cosmic history have ever been the same, so the world is in a constant state of flux. To use a single word or idea as a complete description of the world was therefore inadequate. Instead they propose a view akin to Bohr's complementary idea, whereby a kind of interpenetrating essay of events would need to be prescribed. We must remember that the people we are speaking of were not modern scientists but an ancient society and yet they had the insight to recognise that *everything in nature was flowing from its current state towards its opposite.* It is this constant pouring out of pure possibility that drives the cosmos to change from day to night, summer to winter and life to death.

They observed the cyclic pattern of all things in nature – rivers become clouds only to become rivers once more; stars die only to give rise to life on planets like ours; we give life to the next generation only to give it up ourselves. Nothing in nature stands alone; all is interconnected in the web of consciousness. What we perceive is being created by own our eyes and ears and yet it is only because there is something for us to describe other than ourselves that we can ever say that we are anything at all. To be human is to be what a tree is not; it is to do what a lion or an elephant does not. We can only define ourselves in relation to everything else and, therefore, much as we create the world though our senses, it too creates us.

It is this interdependency of all things that the Tai-Chi symbol expresses. The term 'yin-yang' which is synonymous with Tai-Chi attempts to represent the symbol in text. It does so by insisting that the two words be written without the word 'and' between them – 'yin and yang' would imply a separation, the likes of which the ancient Chinese sought to avoid. With yin-yang, they are saying that what is being described must always be a function of its opposite and yet it can allude to being separateness too.

In the case of the symbol itself, the two shapes, are often described as fish, swimming around each other. The symbol is intended to simulate a sense of movement with a cyclic motivation. Each of the two colours are dissolving into each other, which represents the notion that the world is neither this nor that but both at the same time and yet somehow it is dualistic too. To the Western mind this is the same paradox we face in physics today but to Bohr and the Taoists this is the way the world is and what is needed is an adequate means of expressing it. To illustrate this, the black fish has a white eye and the white fish has a black eye, which represents the notion that everything holds the seed of its opposite and so there is this constant flow of all things away from what they are towards their opposite.

This sets up a constant gradient away from how things are towards an opposing state, which can never reach a conclusion either as this also contains the seed of its opposite and so must flow back along the implied gradient. This leads to a world that is in a constant state of movement, driven not by something solid and reducible but by the more arbitrary notion of an idea. It is this very concept of all things being an expression of their opposite that lies at the seat of creation. The Taoists say that it is the nothingness that creates everything and likewise it is because there is everything that we can perceive the concept of nothingness.

This is a difficult notion for us to grasp as we are fixated on the notion of the world being made of something solid. When we think about what energy might be made of, our instinct points towards some kind of substance, but the Chinese believe that the life force of the cosmos, what they call chi, does not have a tangible presence and can only ever be witnessed in how it affects matter. They accept that it is arbitrary and can never be described by ordinary verbs and nouns and so one must evolve one's language away from the chains of classic dualism.

Beyond the Paradox

My friend Tim Freke has written a superb essay on this syntactical transition. In his book *The Mystery Experience,* he introduces the term paradox-logical or 'paralogical'. He claims that in describing the world, it should not be a case of 'either/or' but rather 'both/and'. Our example of the wave/particle problem now becomes both a wave and a particle; it is also neither a wave nor a particle and it can also be a wave or a particle. It depends on how we are willing to look at it. We are talking about a revolution of language and the emerging frame is, paralogically, not a frame at all, for it seeks to abandon the idea of reduction.

The ability to see the world as separate and also as one has been spoken of for centuries by the various mystics of the world. Buddhism and Hinduism celebrate this state of the enlightened mind. To know the world as it is, according to Eastern philosophy, is to see one's own self in all. The illusion of separation is what precipitates the paradox. The notion that the other is exclusive of the self is false because there is no self without the other – the two are mutually interdependent. This is what we come to realise when we wake up to the oneness of everything.

To see the world in such a light is not an intellectual achievement, nor is it some a deep understanding of the mathematics of quantum entanglement. The knowing of all as one and yet separate too and the ability to transcend this paradox is a far more subtle affair. One still sees the world as it is, but can let go the need to describe it, as one knows that everything is everything because there is nothing we can describe without considering every other thing it is not. A sense of relief fills the mind, as old ideas dissolve into the matrix of all things.

One often finds that symbol and metaphor is the best way to describe the enlightened state because if we say, 'It is this' or 'It is that', we are implying what it is not and if we do this, we will have turned it into just another concept. Any concept used to describe this state will ultimately fall short because it is no particular thing and yet it is everything. We can think of how mathematicians might describe such a condition: they might consider infinity as a means to explore it. To be infinite is to be all possible things at the same time and therefore it is to be non-definable as one thing or another, which is to be non-finite or undefined. We could say that if everything is the same thing then nothing actually exists as there would be no sense of discrimination between things and thus no-thing. And yet this would not deny the existence of all things, which could still prevail, but only as temporary fixtures, as anything that does exist could not be permanent in a world that is propelled by the thrust of infinity.

I liken the linguistic difficulties here to seeing the world with one eye – on the surface everything appears the same as if one was using two eyes, but when we do use two eyes we attain the perception of depth. Likewise, I suggest that when we view the world through ordinary dualistic language, it feels adequate but when we adopt the non-dualistic approach, we can wake up to an entirely different world. When I say, 'I am having a lucid dream', what I actually mean is that I see the dream the same way as it was before, but now I have shifted my own internal perception of the event, which I have achieved by engaging a language frame which allows for me to be both the person in the room and the room that contains the person at the same time.

This is the essence of lucid dreaming: to be able to see beyond the surface of your circumstances, to see that although everything in the dream is separate it is also one and that one is you. It takes a certain kind of language to accommodate this and that is the non-dual view of reality, which allows the critical function to ease off its constant need to rationalise the world. By knowing that you are both the dreamer and the dream, you can gain control of the dream. This ability to make magic happen in the dream becomes as natural as moving your body; you decide what you want to happen and will it to be so. If you want to fly, you fly. Dreaming is ultimately you interacting with your own expanded self.

Even if you have never had a lucid dream, you can still understand what I am suggesting: as both the dreamer and the dream, what you conceive becomes your reality. But as any of us lucid dreamers will tell you, the truth is that we are all too often lost in the illusion of separation to truly grasp the unity of the dream consciousness. Even though we are aware of the fact that we are dreaming, we still interact with other dream beings as if they were normal people just like you and I. And in a sense they are, as they seem perfectly able to operate their world, in the same way that we do. They seem emotional, intelligent and even opinionated at times. Their behaviour is so complex that one cannot help but feel they have an autonomous nature.

I have often wondered about other beings in the dream and how they might perceive their reality. My own experience has revealed them to be frequently unable to corroborate my own view of my circumstances. They rarely agree that what we are experiencing is a dream and I even once had a dream being pick a fight with me when I suggested this. One might speculate that, if they are aspects of my own self, there is also an internal conflict in my own thinking about my circumstances. Perhaps, as conventional psychology would suggest, their denial of the dream demonstrates a deeper disbelief of my own. Even when I know I am dreaming I can still treat the world as physical. I might climb stairs or open doors or even take change out of my pocket to pay for something in a dream, but why? After all, isn't this all my dream of me?

The same psychological dilemma arises from the psychedelic experience. I am persuaded by the voice in the head that what I have entered into is a communion with another sentient being. I try to debate the possibility that I am experiencing just another aspect of my own consciousness, only to be cut off by the voice that claims to be the spirit of the plant or some alien being from another dimension. It insists that I pay attention as I am instructed about the subtle nuances of my reality. I assume, once more, the role of the student allowing the teacher to take control. To have this experience first-hand is to know it to be true. All of the intellectual models we have of reality are swept aside to make way for the voice that enters the mind. One cannot help but feel humbled deeply by the profound wisdom of the deity-like other.

So where do you end and where does the world begin? The world 'out there' is only ever heard by our ears and seen through our eyes. It is there only when we are aware enough to notice it. So how can we really talk about separation when everything is entangled in our senses and written in our words? Perhaps the ultimate mystery of our being is that we are all individuals in our own right, but at a deeper level, we are one universe subjectively interacting with and complexifying itself in every passing moment. Our task, it seems, is to understand this in our everyday lives and for this we need to upgrade our linguistic construct from the dogma of dualistic paradox to paralogical prose of pure possibility.

I therefore want to propose a new definition of a lucid dream, which couches language right at the metaphysical centre: 'Lucid dreaming is when matter realises it is mind and takes on a new creative perception.' In the critical state of consciousness reality is organised into a tight system of strict laws, which can be empirically evaluated to produce predictable outcomes. The semi-critical state, by contrast, is ordained by a coherent dismantling of the self. Although this may seem like an oxymoron, it is when matter says to itself 'I am mind' that it liberates itself from the conformity of physical restriction. To make music fill your ears in the ordinary world, you'd need an instrument to vibrate the air molecules and make your eardrums dance accordingly, but in a lucid dream you could simply shout out your desire to the dream and a symphony will saturate your senses.

As we venture off into the future, one can begin to conceive of an alchemical fantasy in which spirit has been completely distilled from matter. Virtual realities fuelled by quantum computing may one day yield a world that is indistinguishable from a dream. The lucid dreamer has already stepped into this world of pure creative possibility, where the infinity of self and other are both the same and different; it is a place where here is there and far is near; a world where all is one and that union is the dream of you and me.

The altruistic glue that holds the cosmos together has long been the concern of poets and philosophers alike but one does not ordinarily consider it to the be the concern of the scientist. However, it never fails to satisfy me that the most important question Einstein felt we could ask of the cosmos was whether or not it was a friendly place. One night, upon realising that I was dreaming, I took it upon myself to converse with the cosmos. I would be the self and it would be the other and together we would be the all-encompassing dream. I stared into a vast naked sky, filled my lungs with intention and shouted, 'Is the universe a friendly place?'

The sky, as I recall, was that shade of blue we are so rarely treated to: a majestic clarity unspoilt by even a single cloud. And yet something insisted that it would not go unnoticed against the perfect canvas: a perfectly bright star. Several more stars began to shine against the virgin canvas and as I looked on in wonder the sky and stars began to swirl. Soon the rest of the dream did too, including me. I was whisked up into this perfect storm of cosmic colours and spread like butter across the whirling sky. Everything became intensely bright and warm and began to glow like some brilliant luminous vibrating energy. I had lost any sense of my own body and could no longer perceive of here or there. I had completely dissolved into the dream and I was vibrating with the most intense, orgasmic sensation I have ever felt.

The feeling became so overwhelming that I (or what was left of me) could no longer take it and so I returned to my reality, shooting upright in my bed. I was relieved, thrilled and perplexed at the same time. It was terrifying to have lost myself and yet it felt safe and familiar, like one had returned to the womb of creation itself. What had I experienced? I could not say for sure but it felt beyond conceptual language. I would do the feelings I experienced a disservice by trying to describe them and yet I am compelled to share them as best I can. An overwhelming sense that everything is always OK even when it feels otherwise, pervaded my mind. I felt the deep connection between all things and a boundlessness of time. Everything seemed eternal. For me the world would never be the same. I was certain of something so much bigger than me, something so much more powerful that I could only describe as magic.

If the world we occupy is truly boundless, then what can we say about the process of death? Perhaps the ultimate mystery of death is wrapped up in our beginning. In that same paralogic way that darkness creates light and left creates right, death might in fact be the seed of life. It is through the death of the self, as we know it, that the door opens for another to be born. To speak of life after death would therefore be to talk of here and now. The clock keeps ticking but it is only ever the present moment that we know and 'I', the observer, is always at the centre of it. Death is a certainty; so is life. But the question remains: who are you really?

Between the opposites, behind the thoughts in the eternal dimension of now, there lies a special lexicon which has the capacity to contain all things. It was the first tone to be uttered and that which speaks with all of the syllables that fill our world today. It is boundless in dimension because it takes no form and makes no sound. Words are only ever an expression of what they are not and what is never anything is therefore all things at the same time. For it is emptiness that creates the space to hold the form, in the same way that it is stillness that allows for the movement to be made. Therefore, it is the opposite of language that creates all things and yet there are so many words to describe it – some call it God, others call it the source, but I prefer the beauty and wonder of pure silence.

Lightning Source UK Ltd.
Milton Keynes UK
UKOW01f1326090616

275954UK00002B/327/P